FINDIN

*Stories of the men, women and children
who fled to Wales to escape the Nazis*

FINDING REFUGE

*Stories of the men, women and children
who fled to Wales to escape the Nazis*

Andrea Hammel

HONNO PRESS

First published in Great Britain in 2022 by Honno Press
D41 Hugh Owen Building, Penglais Campus, Aberystwyth University,
Aberystwyth, SY23 3DY

1 2 3 4 5 6 7 8 9 10

A catalogue record for this book is available from the British Library.

Published with the financial support of the Books Council of Wales.

ISBN (paperback) 978-1-912905-68-3
ISBN (ebook) 978-1-912905-69-0
Cover design: Sion Ilar/Books Council of Wales
Text design: Elaine Sharples
Printed by: 4Edge

To Winifred V. Davies and all my Welsh friends

CONTENTS

INTRODUCTION

Why write this book?

I came to live in Wales in 2010 and I have lived in Aberystwyth ever since and, all things being equal, I have no intention of leaving again for any length of time. Coming to a new place, where I did not know anyone besides one academic colleague I had briefly encountered at a conference, makes you see a society and a place with new eyes. A lot of what I thought I knew about Wales was probably wrong.

I was born in West Germany in 1968. Looking at my birthdate in 2021 it looks much closer to the Nazi regime, the Second World War and the Holocaust than it felt like during my childhood and youth. My parents were only in their early 20s when I was born and had both been born just after 1945. While other Germans of my generation report an eerie silence in their families about the crimes of National Socialist Germany and its people, I had had long searching discussions with mine. My family were Protestants and my family history includes women and men who both opposed and supported the National Socialist Party and the Nazi regime. One of my great-grandfathers was a miner and an active member of the Social Democratic Party. (While clearing out my parents' house, I found the letter of congratulations for being a member of the SPD for 40 years issued in 1950.) Early on during the Nazi period, he was sent to prison for five weeks by the local magistrates' court for making anti-Nazi speeches and lost his job as a result. Another great-grandfather worked as a porter at the local university and was given the choice of either becoming a member of the Nazi party or losing his job. He decided to join. My grandmother, the daughter of the Social Democratic miner, once told me a story where she described carrying the suitcase of a local elderly Jewish woman, whose family had left (fled?) Germany, to the station. I was too young or too stupid to ask my grandmother where she thought this woman was going. From a young age the historical responsibility of being German after the Holocaust weighed heavily on me.

I came to Britain in 1988. West Germany felt small and parochial and I was looking for something new. I was looking for an adventure. I was looking for somewhere with a different history. Britain felt exciting and cosmopolitan because of its multiculturalism. I liked the English language and I lived in London for a year but then decided to stay on to go to university which at the time was possible as Britain was in the EU and tuition fees did not need to be paid by the individual student.

After completing undergraduate and postgraduate studies at Essex and Sussex Universities, I was interested in writing a PhD thesis. Some academics claim that you always write a little bit about yourself. I am not sure about this theory, but I was interested in the points where German and British culture met and interacted. At the same time, I wanted to rehabilitate those who had to flee Germany and resettle in the UK. I wrote about five women novelists who had to flee from Nazi Germany and Austria and eventually settled in the UK. I have researched refugees from National Socialism ever since, and the subject has proven more relevant to contemporary life than I initially thought.

So, given my long residence in the country and the focus of my working life, it seemed a natural development to write about refugees from National Socialism in Wales. But there are further urgent reasons that have led me to write this book and write it now. Since the Mediterranean refugee crisis came to attention of the Northern European media, in 2015, and refugees from the Ukraine arriving in 2022, comparisons are often made between refugees fleeing to the UK now and those that fled to the UK in the past. This link is important, and complicated at the same time. Researching the history of refugees has certainly had an impact on me personally: for a number of years now, I have been part of a

2

charity called Aberaid that helps refugees (from Syria, Afghanistan and Ukraine for example) locally and internationally. I feel that we need to learn from history for the future, but to do so we need to know more about the stories of the past.

I want to tell the stories of the men, women and children who fled to Wales over 80 years ago to escape the Nazis, to show the challenges they faced as well as highlight their achievements. I also want to explore the fact that Wales has been a nation providing sanctuary for refugees for a long time. Wales is a nation that is far less homogenous than some think, because of migration and as a result of previous welcomes to refugee peoples. There has been research on the multicultural communities of Tiger Bay in Cardiff and on the Belgian First World War refugees in Rhyl. This book will tell another set of stories about refugees from Nazism.

I feel that only by accepting this complexity can Wales move forward. I am a migrant, I came to Wales and made it my home; many refugees came to Wales under much more challenging circumstances and made it their home. We do not exactly know how many refugees from Nazism settled in Wales. It might have been as many as 2,000 individuals, all with their unique stories. I have chosen to write about individuals with different experiences such as child refugees who arrived on their own, those who arrived in family groups, artists and industrialists.

Fleeing National Socialism

Following the National Socialist Party's assumption of power in January 1933, and Adolf Hitler's appointment as chancellor of Germany, life became very difficult for German citizens and residents who were not considered 'Aryan' or who could be identified as political opponents of the new regime. The Nazis managed to eradicate all democratic processes very quickly and took over most institutions, which had a devastating effect on the lives of Jews and political opponents. Members of the political opposition, even Members of Parliament, as well as journalists and writers who had previously spoken out against National Socialist doctrine, immediately found themselves in a dangerous position. Other persecuted groups included Sinti and Romani travellers, homosexuals and Jehovah's Witnesses. Many were imprisoned, some violently attacked and even killed, and many sought to escape.

The pace of emigration after 1933 was essentially driven by National Socialist government policy. Jewish professionals were no longer allowed to practise law or medicine – or at best allowed only to work with Jewish clients or patients – and were excluded from the civil service. The threat toward the Jewish population became even more acute after the passing of the 1935 Nuremberg Laws, in which citizens were classified according to 'racial' ancestry. Categorisation as Jewish or 'non-Aryan' had little to do with religious conviction or self-identification. According to National Socialist ideology, a person was considered Jewish if they had one Jewish grandparent. This meant that some Germans, who had not even known that they had Jewish antecedents and had grown up in the Christian faith, were considered Jewish and excluded from public and professional life in Germany. Those considered Jewish were also given an inferior legal status in society. Such policies meant that many were excluded from schools and universities, and adults and children of Jewish descent were excluded from many public places such as parks, cinemas and swimming pools. Jewish shop and business owners first lost their customers or clients, and ultimately their shops and businesses. The Nazi authorities encouraged the takeover of Jewish shops and businesses by 'Aryan' Germans and many former competitors and employees quickly exploited the situation and ousted their former colleagues, bosses and neighbours, effectively stealing their livelihoods from them. The 'non-Aryan' shop and business owners were not compensated.

The Nazis wanted to remove all political opponents and 'non-Aryan' people from Germany. During the 1930s, the Nazi authorities had nothing against such people leaving Germany, and even facilitated their emigration to a certain extent. However, as much as they wanted 'non-Aryan' people to leave, they did not want them to take any assets or money with them. This made it extremely difficult for many families to find refuge as most countries placed financial qualifications on who was considered worthy of admittance at that time. Jewish people without money or assets often found themselves at the bottom of the list of desirable immigrants. Therefore, Jewish families in Germany became increasingly desperate as they queued at embassies and consulates, contacted relatives, friends and acquaintances who lived abroad, and searched for possible routes and destinations. Some got lucky and discovered someone they knew who would vouch for them or put up the required sum of money to allow them to obtain a visa. Of course, not all Jewish families wanted to emigrate. There was still a sizable proportion, even after 1935, who assumed that it would all 'blow over': either the Nazis would be forced out of power, or their antisemitic stance would somehow soften. After all, the Jews of Europe were used to discrimination and persecution ranging from religious antisemitism in Western Europe in the Middle Ages, including the banishing of all Jews from England in 1290, to the frequent pogroms in the Russian Empire and Eastern Europe at the end of the 19th and beginning of the 20th century.

Of those that did manage to leave 1930s Germany, many moved to neighbouring countries such as the Netherlands (which is what Anne Frank's family did) or France, or even Austria. However, Nazi persecution policies caught up with those who had tried to escape to Austria on 12 March 1938, when the German Reich annexed Austria and Hitler drove triumphantly through Vienna, cheered by the thousands of Austrians who supported his policies. After Germany invaded, the Netherlands and France would also later turn out to be far from safe for Jews.

The November Pogrom on 9 and 10 November 1938, also sometimes called 'Kristallnacht' on account of the broken glass visible in the streets of Germany and the annexed Austrian territory, was the turning point for many Jewish citizens. During these days of state-sponsored violence, it must have become clear to everyone that Jews would not be able to continue living in the Reich at all, and many feared for their lives. Many Jewish men were arrested and incarcerated in concentration camps. A large number of Jewish people lost their lives, although not on the scale of the genocidal mass murder that would be perpetrated after 1941 in the Holocaust, also known as the Shoah.

Seeking sanctuary

The UK government's immigration policy underwent dramatic changes during the first 40 years of the 20th century. The Aliens Act of 1905 was designed to address what was seen at time as 'the influx' of Eastern European Jews having to flee the pogroms in Eastern Europe and the Russian Empire. Large-scale immigration of impoverished Jews was seen as a threat to the finances and the religious harmony of the UK. The 1905 Aliens Act may be considered as the first step on the path to a modern immigration control system. The Aliens Restriction Acts of 1914 and 1919, which bookended the First World War, further limited the rights of immigrants to enter the UK. From that point onwards, until Britain signed up to the 1951 Refugee Convention, refugees lost specific legal protection and were treated like any other immigrants, admitted only on a case-by-case basis. The main consideration taken into account by immigration officials was whether the person seeking entry was considered to be of benefit to the British state. There seems to have been some room for leniency and individual officials did make decisions on humanitarian grounds after 1919, and even after 1933. This bending of the rules ranged from border officials at Dover overlooking incomplete paperwork to the large-scale granting of visas to Jewish applicants in Berlin by the British Secret Intelligence Officer at the UK embassy in Berlin, Major Frank Foley. Those rescued in this way include the family of Michael Mamelok, father-in-law of the late Tory MP James Brokenshire.

However, as a rule the UK government embraced the policy of trying as much as possible to place the financial and organisational burden of refugees on non-governmental agencies, religious communities and charities. After 1933, the Jewish organisations of the UK financially underwrote the admittance of Jewish refugees from the German Reich and administered their care and support. This was obviously a great responsibility and a monumental task.

Research in this field is not always able to provide reliable numbers as the record keeping of the UK government is patchy. We believe that between 1933 and March 1938 the numbers of those seeking refuge were not as large as later, which made the ad hoc arrangements that evolved just about workable. It is estimated that about 4,500 refugees fled to the UK between 1933 and 1935, and a further 5,500 by March 1938, when the German Reich annexed Austria. From this point of time onwards, especially after the November Pogrom of 1938, the number of those trying to escape increased manyfold. An additional 80,000 refugees had entered the UK by the beginning of the Second World War in September 1939. Not all, but a very large majority of the refugees were Jewish. In comparison, in 2015 the UK government agreed to resettle 20,000 refugees fleeing the conflict in Syria via the Vulnerable Persons Resettlement Scheme in the UK within five years.

Of the roughly 90,000 refugees who reached UK, around 12,000 individuals then migrated further and settled in other countries. However, this still meant that about 78,000 refugees from National Socialism were living in the UK by September 1939 (of whom around 30,000 had come from Austria). This is probably an underestimation as children who entered with their parents were put on the same visa and not counted separately. Needless to say, we know very little about the number and the nature of those who were unsuccessful in their applications to escape and find refuge in the UK. What we can say with certainty is that a very large number of people were unsuccessful in their attempt to flee , and many of them were later murdered in the Holocaust.

Because of the rapid increase in applications after March 1938, when thousands of Austrian Jews sought to escape in a short space of time, the UK government introduced even more restrictive policies. With the tacit consent of the Anglo-Jewish community, who clearly feared that they would not be able to support more refugees, the government introduced new visa requirements making finding refuge in Britain more difficult. Fears regarding the state of the labour market and rising antisemitism played a part in this implementation of ever more stringent restrictions. The negative attitude towards Continental refugees was fuelled by xenophobic newspapers, certain sections of the government and far right groups. There was, however, also a sizable number of UK citizens who were very sympathetic towards the plight of those persecuted by National Socialism and who continued to campaign for the rescue of more refugees. The details and consequences of the November Pogrom of 1938 were widely reported in British press and raised awareness and sympathy with the wider British public.

There were four main categories under which one could apply for a visa to Britain. First, the UK government was willing to admit world-famous artists, scientists or academics. Amongst these renowned arrivals was the Viennese psychoanalyst Sigmund Freud, who arrived in London on 6 June 1938, with eleven members of his family – and his dog.

A second route to gaining a visa was to be able to convince the UK authorities that you had the assets and the expertise to set up a viable business. Those with expertise in manufacturing were preferred, but they had to be able to convince the authorities that their UK business would be able to create jobs for UK workers. If the refugee industrialists were willing to set up businesses in the so-called Special Areas – deprived areas such as South Wales, Tyneside, Cumberland and Lanarkshire, with a high unemployment rate and ear-marked for extra investment – this counted further in their favour.

For the less well known or the less wealthy, it was not easy to gain admittance: the applications of many well-qualified professionals such as physicians or lawyers were rejected. Professional organisations in these fields lobbied the government against a generous admissions policy as they feared competition from professional Continental refugees. If a qualified doctor managed to flee to the UK via a different route, he or she would not normally be allowed to practise for some time and would be made to retake their qualifications.

If the refugee was willing to work in a field where there was a labour shortage it was also possible that they would be granted a visa. Domestic service was one such field. In the late 1930s. the UK was said to be suffering from a 'servant crisis' as fewer and fewer young women wanted to take on such work. The pay was very low and the conditions and hours even worse; domestic servants often were expected to be available all day and were allowed very little time off. They were usually required to live in the households of their employer and were not allowed to have their dependants live with them. As there was a serious shortage of UK applicants for these jobs, the government therefore issued so-called 'Domestic Permits' to any Continental refugee who was able to show that they had found employment as a domestic in the UK. Around 20,000 mainly female refugees managed to flee to the UK via this scheme. Psychiatric care and certain agricultural jobs were also considered under a similar but much more limited scheme.

Finally, there were also different rules for refugees under the age of 18. Around 10,000 unaccompanied minors fled to the UK on the so-called 'Kindertransport'. This functioned as a visa waiver scheme and was in place between December 1938 and September 1939. Today the Kindertransport is one of the better-known policies enabling refugees to flee to the UK in the 1930s. The scheme is often celebrated, but there are a number of myths that should be debunked in relation to the Kindertransport. To start with, it was mainly individuals and charities that assisted with the organisation and the financial support of the scheme, and not the

British government. Most Kindertransportees were not orphans as is sometimes assumed; they left their parents and families behind, not because they didn't want to leave too, but because the UK government would only admit the children. Chaotic organisation and lack of preparation and support caused many of the young refugees harm, even after they arrived in the relative safety of the UK. Kindertransportees were placed in foster families all over the UK, including in Wales. Some of the teenage refugees were accommodated in communal settings. These were sometimes organised by Zionist organisations whose aim was to prepare the young people for eventual emigration to Palestine. Llandough Castle in the Vale of Glamorgan and Gwrych Castle near Abergele were two of the locations for such training centres – or *hachsharot* – and, with up to 180 residents, Gwrych Castle was the largest in the UK.

Fleeing on a Kindertransport

The events of 9 November 1938 meant that both Jewish families on the Continent and the UK government were pushed to consider measures they had not been able to bring themselves to agree to before. Until then, most families had not been willing to consider parting from their children, but after the November Pogrom parents felt that if they could not escape and find refuge together, they should at least try to find an escape route for their children.

For the UK government, it was public pressure after 9 November 1938 – from its citizens horrified to read about the violent attacks on the Continental Jews – that pushed them into action. The violence perpetrated against the Jewish population had been reported extensively in British papers and on the radio. Many British people were outraged and demanded that their government ought to help Continental Jews. At a Cabinet Committee Meeting discussion on 14 November 1938, various possible reactions to the events were discussed and Prime Minister Neville Chamberlain stated that 'something effective should be done to alleviate the terrible fate of the Jews in Germany.' He alluded to the public mood and acknowledged that there was a certain pressure on the government to be seen to be doing something. However, although various suggestions for helping the German Jews leave Germany were discussed, none was decided on during this particular meeting. The next day, a group of Anglo-Jewish leaders met with Prime Minister Chamberlain and the idea of temporarily admitting a number of unaccompanied children for the purpose of training and education was discussed. Just a week later, the Home Secretary, Sir Samuel Hoare, announced the government's new refugee policy, which included the directive that all children whose maintenance could be guaranteed by private individuals or charitable organisations were allowed to be admitted to Britain without going through the arduous process of applying for a visa. This was the official go-ahead for the Kindertransport. (The term Kindertransport in the singular is normally used for the scheme that brought around 10,000 children to the UK. Used in the plural Kindertransports can refer to individual trains that brought over a certain number at any one time, though some groups were brought to the UK by ship or plane.)

Public pressure was instrumental in pushing a formerly reluctant government to make this decision. However, it is clear that the British government was only willing to support such a change of policy if it did not have to commit financial resources to the initiative. In this respect, the government only partially backed the scheme, enabling but not funding it. The decision to admit children without their families was a momentous one. The exact reasons are disputed but we know that the government was worried about the high unemployment rate at the time, and some argued that letting large numbers of adult refugees into the UK would increase the number of unemployed workers. This would not be the case when admitting child refugees as in most cases it would be many years before they would need a job.

Those who worried that some of the Continental refugees might be spies or might agitate against the UK would also be less concerned if the UK just admitted minors. Children would also be less visible in the community, especially if they were accommodated in foster families, and thus there would be less occasion for antisemitic sentiments to arise. Again, we do not have exact numbers, but it is estimated that at least three quarters of those who fled on a Kindertransport left their parents behind on the Continent.

Many children understood the reasons why their parents wanted them to leave their home and family without them, as they had experienced increasing persecution and often even violence first hand. Some nevertheless could not help feelings of abandonment or guilt as if their separation from their parents had somehow been their fault.

Most of us cannot even imagine how the parents of the Kindertransportees must have felt when parting from their children. Some child refugees were told by their parents that the parents would follow them to Britain or emigrate themselves and send for the children after a period of a few months' separation. Although it is possible that in some cases this was told to the children to alleviate their anxiety about being separated from their families, letters from the parents show that this was often their intention even if the end they were unable to achieve it. The parents of twelve-year-old Eva Mosbacher from Thuringia in Germany include precise descriptions of their emigration attempts and the efforts to get visas but also record the challenge: 'I know that no one is really keen to have us neither here nor there, but we have no choice but to try everything to emigrate anywhere possible.'

In other cases, parents tried to put their children on a Kindertransport because they had managed to obtain a visa for themselves and intended to keep the family together. As discussed previously, one way of gaining a visa and work permit to the UK was to find employment as a domestic servant. The Jewish community in Vienna had pre-printed application forms on which parents could state that they had obtained a domestic permit to enter the UK and thus wished their child to be considered for a Kindertransport. Clearly parents wanted their children to be in the same country as them, possibly hoping for a speedy reunion. This worked out for some families but in the case of those who did work as domestic staff, their employers saw them as employees first and foremost and were often not sensitive to their situation. Most were not allowed to have their children live with them in the household of their employers. In other cases, the economically difficult circumstances and limited accommodation dictated that child refugees could not live with their parents, even if they had all resettled in Britain. This was the case with the Dienemann family: the children escaped on a Kindertransport in January 1939 and the parents in summer of the same year but the children were not able to join their parents in Oxford because of money and accommodation worries and continued to stay in their foster families.

As discussed, the eruption of violence towards the Jewish population in Germany during the November Pogroms of 1938 was not only a turning point for German Jewish organisations and individuals, it also showed the international community that the German Jews were in an absolutely desperate situation. The speed at which it was put in place and the scale of the Kindertransport are two of the key reasons why it is often mentioned with admiration, but this admiration needs qualification. Neither rapid emigration of large numbers of people nor child immigration to Britain were without precedent. During the First World War, a large number of Belgian refugees were admitted and during the Spanish Civil War of 1936–9, about 4,000 unaccompanied Basque children found refuge in the UK.

The speed with which the Kindertransport was set up meant that no or hardly any vetting or preparation of the children's eventual placements were possible, which had dire consequences for some Kindertransportees who either had to change placements often or found themselves living in damaging situations. Nevertheless, the fact that it was less than two weeks between the decision to admit unaccompanied child refugees in late November 1938 and the arrival of a ferry on 2 December 1938 at Harwich with around 200 child refugees on board shows the determination and rapidly effective organisational skills of all involved.

During the ten months between December 1938 and September 1939, transports arrived from Germany, Austria, Czechoslovakia and Poland. On the German side, a Department for Child Emigration had already been established by the Reich's Deputation of the German Jews in 1933. Until then, only individual children or small groups of children had emigrated, for example to France. But the existence of an organisational structure meant that there were people with experience available, who could step up to deal with the formalities and organisation of a large group of Jewish children to be sent to the UK. In Austria, the situation was different, as there had been no communal initiative to send unaccompanied children abroad before the Annexation of Austria in March 1938, which made the helpers less experienced. The fact that the Jewish population in Austria was concentrated mainly in Vienna made their challenge a little easier. In Germany, the Department for Child Emigration, which had its offices in Berlin, collected all the applications from Berlin itself and from provincial Jewish organisations and community offices located all over Germany. The Department pre-selected the applications and sent them on to London, where the Refugee Children's Movement (RCM) had its headquarters in Bloomsbury House in London. Here the children who were deemed to be suitable for emigration were chosen and this was then communicated back to the organisations on the Continent. The children and their parents were subsequently informed of the decision and were notified of their likely departure date. They were allowed to take two small pieces of luggage, which had to be labelled and had to be light enough to be able to be carried by the children themselves. No valuables and only a small amount of money was allowed to be taken out of Germany. The age of the children ranged from two to seventeen, though there were some reports of even younger children travelling.

Trains left from larger cities such as Berlin or Frankfurt am Main and the children were either asked to board the trains there or picked up at stations on route. A small number of adults acted as guardians to the children on the train and supervised them. These adults were required to return to Germany or Austria after completing their task and there are no reports that any individual did not do so. The most likely route from Germany to the UK was via Bentheim and the Dutch Hoek of Holland, where the parties boarded the ferry to Harwich. There were also transports that took the train route to Hamburg or Bremen and from there a boat to Southampton. Upon arrival in the UK, the children were either put in holding camps - a number of empty holiday camps in East Anglia had been put at the RCM's disposal, the largest being Dovercourt - or transferred straight onto trains to London, either arriving at London Liverpool Street Station or Victoria Station. Eventually children were either accommodated in hostels, in boarding schools or with foster families. On 25 November 1938, the BBC broadcast the first call for foster parents in Britain and this elicited 500 immediate responses from those willing to accommodate children. There is little evidence that the number of Kindertransportees was ever limited by a lack of foster parents during the ten-month duration of the scheme, which is astonishing. However, as discussed before there was little or no vetting of these volunteers.

The decision by the British government to admit only unaccompanied child refugees on the Kindertransport has been scrutinised by many. There was clearly pressure from the public and the media to select refugees that would not immediately seek employment and thus potentially disadvantage unemployed British citizens. This can also be seen as a reason behind the decision to only give work permits to those who were willing to work in jobs that were not attracting British applicants such as domestic work or nursing. Furthermore, it is clear that British society and British politics suffered from its fair share of antisemitism. In the conclusion to her book, *Whitehall and the Jews*, Louise London quotes the antisemitic opinions of politicians, officials and ordinary citizens and comments that 'moderate indulgence in social anti-Jewish prejudice was so widespread as to be unremarkable.' Adult refugees, especially adult males, were seen as threatening. Child refugees, however, did not have the same negative connotations and could also be imagined as readily assimilating to the British way of life. The pictures of child refugees that were published in newspapers of the time reflect an image of the children as sweet and innocent. However, it might be argued that portraying child refugees as innocent, suggests that adult refugees are somehow guilty and deserving of persecution. Placing the child refugees with foster parents also had the advantage that they were dispersed around the country and not likely to be visible in large numbers to those who were critical of Jewish refugees coming to the UK.

Many more families wished to put their children forward for inclusion on a Kindertransport to the UK than there was capacity for. In the beginning of the Kindertransport movement a sizeable number of children were selected according to the urgency of them having to escape Nazi persecution, i.e. boys between fifteen and seventeen years old were seen as particularly urgent cases as they were at danger of arrest. Also, children who were living in Jewish children's homes were perceived to be priority cases as this sort of group accommodation was easily identifiable by those wishing to carry out violent acts. Other urgent cases were those living without one or both of their parents and those in particularly straitened circumstances. The decision-making process was made more difficult by the preference of some British foster parents who asked for girls aged between six and ten. Not finding evidence of overt bias does not mean that it was not more difficult for children from certain backgrounds to emigrate. First, the parents had to have the initiative to seek a place on a Kindertransport. Secondly, as most

British foster families were not Jewish, many of the parents were asked to sign a permission form to allow their children to be placed in non-Jewish families. Children from families who were not willing to allow this and did not sign the form clearly had diminished chances of finding a placement. Furthermore, the RCM did try and select children who would make a good impression on their British hosts and would thus convince others in Britain to continue taking on foster children and hence enlarge the reach of the scheme. Thus children who had disabilities or whose behavioural problems, such as bed-wetting, were detected by those issuing health certificates, were far less likely to be picked for a transport to Britain.

As discussed, the British government did not commit public funds towards the costs of the Kindertransport. On the contrary, it pushed the financial burden on to private individuals and charities by demanding that every child refugee to be admitted under this scheme should be 'guaranteed', i.e. the sum of £50 had to be put up to indemnify the British government against any cost arising from admitting the child to the UK. Additionally, funds were needed for the actual journey and the upkeep of the children. Some of their German and Austrian birth parents were in a position to pay for travel costs, but many were not. Eleanor Rathbone, an Independent MP who championed the cause of refugees from the Continent, argued in a pamphlet published in 1939, that private charitable appeals would not be sufficient to raise the necessary funds. She argued several million pounds were required and should be provided by the government. The government of the time did not agree to this.

One major source of funds was the Jewish community's pre-existing Jewish Refugees Committee. During the 1930s, the committee raised over £5 million. Another source of funding was the Lord Baldwin Fund for Refugees. Philip Voss, a Jewish barrister and Labour Party activist, was a prime mover in the foundation of this charity. He persuaded Lord Baldwin, the former British prime minister, to lend his name to the fund. Despite being a supporter of appeasement, Lord Baldwin was also keen to support refugees in the UK and in early December 1938 he launched a BBC radio appeal in aid of this new charity. He argued that Jewish children and those of Jewish descent in Germany and Austria faced an existential threat and proclaimed: 'Shall they live? Before it is too late, get them out!' a headline that was also used for the newspaper advertising for the Baldwin Fund. Other prominent individuals such as the Archbishop of Canterbury, Dr Cosmo Lang, and the Roman Catholic Archbishop of Westminster, Cardinal Arthur Hinsley, gave their support to the charity. The Post Office Savings Bank issued special savings stamp books in support of the appeal. Many newspapers, even those like the *Daily Mail* that had a long history of hostility towards refugees, supported the Baldwin Fund which raised over £500,000.

Half of this money was used to finance the immigration of Jewish child refugees. Other guarantors were private individuals who were either the child's prospective foster carers or people prepared to guarantee the upkeep of a child refugee while they were placed elsewhere. Initially, an unspecified number of children sent to Britain did not have an individual guarantor but were supported by a pool of guarantees to be distributed by the RCM as it saw fit. Due to financial constraints, by spring 1939 this pool of guarantees from general funds was restricted to 200 cases, which meant that only if one of the 200 individuals already in the UK was no longer in need of a guarantee, could another child refugee come to Britain funded by that pool. In practice, this meant that from March 1939 onwards, in the majority of cases, only children who had an individual guarantor could enter Britain. This was a significant change in procedure and led to a complicated relationship between the Continental organisations and the RCM. As we have seen, potential guarantors and foster parents in the UK were most keen to foster girls aged between six and ten, which was not the largest or most needy group of child refugees waiting to leave Germany. The RCM forcefully rejected the German and Austrian child refugee departments' requests for further children without individual guarantees to be allowed entry into the UK. In the face of these demands, they responded, 'The Movement for the Transport of Children [sic], again, cannot bring over more unguaranteed children, until those already here have been placed. I regret that it is no use to continue to ask for more help than we are giving, because it is not in our power to grant it.'

Not all children who came to Britain on a Kindertransport were Jewish. About 20 per cent of the Kindertransport child refugees would not have been considered part of the Jewish community before 1933 but were defined as Jewish by the National Socialist regime. At the time, these people were referred to as 'non-Aryan Christians' by both British and German organisations and included children with a combination of Christian and Jewish parents, or grandparents who either had no religious affiliation or were in fact Christians. The Quakers, also known as the Society of Friends, with offices in Berlin and Vienna, and other specific organisations connected to the Protestant and Catholic Churches, assisted this group of children on the Continent. The RCM in Britain was an interdenominational organisation and took care of all the different groups of children. A certain amount of wrangling is reported between the representatives of the different categories of children about the numbers of places allocated to each group.

Because of time pressure, very little effort was made to match up the potential foster families with particular children. This led to many unsuitable situations which ranged from a mismatch of cultural and religious backgrounds between foster families and children, to situations in which the children suffered physical and sexual abuse. Also, as nobody could have predicted the outbreak and course of the Second World War, many foster parents had not realised the length of time they would be required to look after their charges. As the children got older and entered adolescence, their relationship with their foster parents often became more difficult.

In many cases, those who arrived as adolescents were accommodated in hostels with other young refugees. Overall, this seems to have been a preferable option for older Kindertransportees as they felt more comfortable in the company of other young people with a similar background. Some of the older Kindertransportees were very disappointed when they were not allowed to follow the educational path they had originally anticipated. They encountered the prejudiced assumption that a basic education should be 'good enough' for a refugee and the view that they should become financially independent as soon as possible in order to support themselves outside of the Kindertransport initiative. After the outbreak of war, many older Kindertransportees played their part in the British war effort, either joining the army or working in a variety of jobs that were considered useful. There are as many Kindertransport stories as there are Kindertransportees and it seems that it depends on a wide variety of factors how individual Kindertransportees remember the war years and narrate them in the story of their lives.

Although the British government can only be described as a rather reluctant partner in the Kindertransport rescue effort, after 1945 it offered naturalisation to almost all those refugees that had spent the duration of the war in the UK and many of the Kindertransportees who had reached the age of maturity chose to become naturalised.

Finding new homes in Wales

Initially, many adult refugees to the UK wanted to settle near large urban centres in England, close to the larger, more vibrant established Jewish communities. Many had little knowledge of the nations of the United Kingdom, including Wales, before they arrived. But some government schemes urged refugees to settle in specific areas. As mentioned, previously, refugee entrepreneurs were encouraged, or in some cases forced, to establish their factories in the so-called Special Areas, of which there was one in South Wales.

Some resented this and some even initially avoided moving to Wales. Joachim Koppel, for example, commuted for some time from London to the factory he established on the industrial estate at Treforest near Pontypridd, but copies of his alien registration certificate show that he was certainly registered as living in Wales for a period, and probably did so for at least some of that time. Refugee domestics had to live in the household of their employer, and thus had no choice as to the area of their resettlement. Others were allocated to an area where there was a labour shortage affecting certain jobs, such as in the timber industry in the area around Llangollen.

A number of refugees came to Wales almost by accident and stayed because they liked Wales for its beautiful landscape and due to the fact that it was not part of the English mainstream. Certainly, artists and writers such as the painter Josef Herman and Kate Bosse-Griffiths, who became a Welsh speaker, Welsh-language author and Welsh-language campaigner, seem to have been influenced by such sentiments.

Some refugees arrived in Wales because they were evacuated from other areas of the UK. Bea Green was a student at University College London when its Education Department was moved to Aberystwyth. Empty manor houses or even a castle provided the space for whole schools to move to Wales or for new residential hostels for young people to be established. Children who arrived in the UK via the Kindertransport scheme were resettled all over the UK, in England, Scotland, Northern Island and Wales, wherever a placement in a foster family or a residential setting could be found.

We have no reliable answers as to the total number of refugees from National Socialism who resettled in Wales. However, in some cases, we can identify specific groups who came to Wales. For example, it seems that a sizeable number of the particular group of Kindertransportees who fled from Prague in summer 1939 found homes in Wales, such as Renate Collins, Harry Weinberger and Lia Lesser. This might be because they arrived towards the end of the

Kindertransport scheme and other possible placements had already been 'filled', or because the Czech Refugee Committee looked to Wales more than other parts of the UK for foster parents.

The people of Wales are known for their hospitality and warmth. Clearly many individuals in Wales tried to help the refugees who had to leave their Continental homes behind. In telling the story of some of the refugees from National Socialism who came to Wales, this book also tells the story of many Welsh people who were hospitable and kind, and put themselves out to be welcoming and inclusive. Of course, there were also examples of the opposite: of hostile encounters and of people who did not manage to fulfil their duties as carers, which could be especially devastating in the case of unaccompanied minors arriving on a Kindertransport. This book aims to tell as many different stories as possible and to try and represent a range of experiences. Most are complex and contain narratives of escape, rescue, hospitality, and resilience, but also of trauma and loss.

THE STORIES

Small ad in the *Guardian* looking for a foster parent
(© from the collection of Julian Borger)

Robert Borger with his parents (© Julian Borger)

Robert Borger as a youth (© Julian Borger)

'HITLER'S LAST VICTIM':
ROBERT BORGER

Nancy and Reg Bingley, schoolteachers living in Caernarfon, were just two of many generous-spirited individuals and families in Wales who felt that they wanted to personally contribute to saving Continental refugees in need. The Bingleys were members of the Fabian Society and the Labour Party and they believed in international humanitarian and political solidarity. They were willing to work for this goal. As the couple had no children of their own but were experienced foster parents, it was therefore logical that they would opt to take care of a child refugee as a way of helping the persecuted. Their family was home to a number of local foster children, and in 1938 they fostered an eleven-year-old refugee boy from Vienna, Robert Borger. The couple, who lived in a semi-detached pebble-dash council house in Pen y Garth, were themselves of modest means but they made up for any lack of money or material comforts with their insight into the needs of the children they cared for.

Robert Borger, son of Erna and Leo Borger, was fortunate to be fostered by the Bingleys. In Vienna, after the Anschluss on 12 March 1938, things had become rapidly worse for the Borger family. Whereas the lives of German Jewish citizens had become slowly more and more restricted as persecution increased over a number of years, antisemitic persecution in Austria was ramped up over a much shorter time period. In Germany, Adolf Hitler and his Nazi party took power in January 1933, the Nuremberg Race Laws came into force in 1935, and everyday violence against the Jewish citizens culminated in the November Pogrom in 1938. In Austria, there were only months between the annexation by Germany in March 1938, the implementation of the race laws in May, and the violence during the pogrom in November 1938. The lives of many Austrian Jews changed very rapidly.

The Borgers were a Jewish family living in Vienna's Third District and owners of a large shop selling radios and musical instruments. Robert was their only child and the centre of his parents' lives. What has to happen to such a family that they would consider sending their young son to live with strangers in a foreign country? In this case, it was an extremely traumatic incident perpetrated by Nazi thugs: Robert had been snatched off the street by some SA brownshirts, members of a special unit who were often involved in street violence in the early years of the Nazi regime. In a display of power and cruelty, they kidnapped Robert and locked him inside a synagogue. Nobody knew where he was and it took some time to find and free him. This was a truly frightening experience for the boy and clearly caused him great distress. It induced what we would now recognise as post-traumatic stress disorder in Robert. Robert's father Leo was also harassed and – like many other Viennese Jews – had been forced to register his family as Jewish; he was then made to scrub the pavement on his hands and knees by the SA. By August 1938, Erna and Leo had made the tough decision to place an advertisement in the *Manchester Guardian*, in the hope that they could find foster parents for Robert, enabling him to escape to the UK. Such advertisements were not uncommon. On 13 August 1938, the day the Borger's ad appeared, a number of other ads were placed looking for anyone who was willing to give a Continental Jewish child or an adolescent a home. Julian Borger, son of Robert and a current *Guardian* journalist, reckons that the *Manchester Guardian* featured over 60 such ads looking for foster families for minors. These were not unique to this specific newspaper: *The Times* and *The Telegraph* published similar advertisements as did some regional papers and a number of Jewish publications. According to Julian, small ads were the revenue driver of the paper in those days and the ad regarding his father appeared in the tuition section. It was possible for minors to obtain a student visa to the UK if it could be claimed that they were entering the country for educational purposes. The other advantage of an unaccompanied refugee minor leaving the German Reich, without adults accompanying him or her, was the fact that the Reich did not demand the payment of the notorious flight tax which in the case of adult refugees often meant leaving almost all assets behind and becoming a penniless refugee.

The text of the Borgers' ad was short and simple: 'I seek a kind person who will educate my intelligent Boy, aged 11, Viennese of good family'. Whether it was the reference to education that drew the *Guardian*-reading Bingleys to this ad and not any other, we do not know, but they certainly managed to dedicate themselves to educating Robert.

Robert's mother Erna also put out a newspaper ad of her own and in this way managed to obtain a position as a domestic servant. They travelled together on the train from Vienna to the UK, Robert on a student visa and Erna on a domestic visa. The only reason Erna was able to bring Robert was because he was sponsored by the Bingleys. Her employers would not allow him to stay with her in their household and she was only allowed to live and work at the employers' residence stipulated on her visa.

Leo Borger was initially left behind in Vienna, but the Bingleys helped him find employment in a factory in Shrewsbury. Corset Silhouette, an underwear manufacturer, had been started by enterprising refugee industrialists. It is likely that the factory owners claimed that they needed Leo's specialist skills, and thus a visa and work permit was issued. So, Robert, Leo and Erna all managed to flee to the UK but had to live apart and the parents carry out manual jobs, which were very different from their previous occupations. Leo worked at the corset factory in Shrewsbury until retirement. Despite the fragmentation of the family, it must have been a consolation to Leo and Erna that Robert had found such a good foster home, and that his foster parents were able to help him with his education. No doubt they believed that this would give him the best start in the new country.

Initially, Robert's foster father Reg Bingley home-schooled Robert and tutored him in English and Welsh, which meant that Robert could communicate fluently with teachers and classmates alike by the time he entered formal education. Reg Bingley had taught himself a dozen languages and was clearly good at communicating the language learning process. He could probably also imagine how difficult adapting to a new environment could be. Unfortunately, this was not the norm at the time. Many child refugees who sought sanctuary in the UK in the late 1930s were thrown into the deep end regarding schooling. Often neither the child refugees nor their classmates, or their teachers, were prepared for the new situation. One boy who was given a free place at a boarding school was picked up by the headmaster from the train station, having just arrived in the UK, and brought straight to the school. He later described the experience as one of complete shock: 'An hour after my arrival at the school I was sitting in a class in school uniform. I did not understand any English. It was totally bewildering.'

Robert had been severely traumatised by his experience of persecution and violence back in Vienna. The Bingleys had to take the whistle off the kettle as it reminded Robert too much of men in authority with whistles in the streets of Vienna, threatening and arresting Jewish citizens. When the Bingleys' friendly landlord came to their house wanting to take Robert for a walk around the old town of Caernarfon, Robert nearly fainted as he believed that he was to be taken out to be killed. Hence, it was a huge advantage for him to be placed with insightful foster parents who were able to devote a lot of time to him. Reg Bingley knew what it was like to be made to feel an outsider as he suffered from chronic illness, which led to extreme curvature of the spine and caused him to move around almost bent over double. Despite this, he still managed to work as a teacher for a number of years, eventually propping up his feet in such a way that he could still make eye contact with his pupils.

Many memoirs of former refugees portray their educational success. There might be a self-selecting element here, because people with a good education are more likely to write memoirs. But it is also true that many young refugees were very ambitious and keen to concentrate on their education. Robert was especially successful. Aged only 16, he won a scholarship to study at Cardiff University. However, leaving Caernarfon and his supportive foster parents behind at such a young age did not work out. Robert suffered from mental health problems and had to come back to the Bingleys. When he had recovered and was a little older, he started his studies again at nearby Bangor University, this time with great success. He specialised in psychology and became a university lecturer, publishing a number of books and academic papers. Eventually, he was appointed Professor of Psychology at Brunel University in West London. Robert married and had children of his own. He kept in touch with his foster parents and brought his children to visit them frequently. As mentioned before, his son, Julian Borger, would later work as a journalist for the same *Guardian* newspaper that had carried the ad enabling his father to escape National Socialist persecution. Robert was clearly affected by what had happened to him as a boy in Vienna, and while he was able to turn some of his negative experience into positive action – he worked for refugee organisations in France after the war and taught in schools as well as university – at other times it was too much of a burden. Sadly, Robert took his own life in 1983. It fell to Julian to inform Nancy Bingley – Reg had already passed away – and she exclaimed in distress that Robert was 'Hitler's last victim'. Nancy Bingley died in 2015 aged 101 and Julian Borger commemorated the relationship between his late father and his former foster mother while standing at her graveside at Caernarfon cemetery overlooking the Menai Strait. He later wrote about his family history in the *Guardian* in connection with the Mediterranean refugee crisis and argued, 'the greatness of the nation lies buried on that Welsh hillside. Britain's "finest hour" is as much about the generosity of the Bingleys, and thousands like them, as it is about the courage of the Spitfire pilots.'

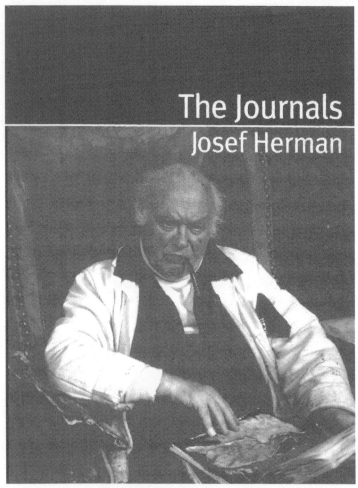

The painter, Josef Herman in later life
(© The Estate of Josef Herman/Halban Publishers)

JOE BACH PAINTING MINERS: THE ARTIST JOSEF HERMAN IN YSTRADGYNLAIS

The painter Josef Herman came to Wales almost by accident but ended up contributing to the cultural life and art of the nation in a significant way. His paintings of working men and women – especially his paintings of the members of the mining community amongst whom he lived for eleven years – bear out an understanding of this way of life that is insightful and timeless. He lived in Ystradgynlais from 1944 to 1955. Born in 1911, Josef's life story is marked by poverty and persecutions, fortunate coincidences, extraordinary talent and the ability to adapt to changing circumstances. Josef was lucky to make friends and find mentors at the right time, helping his development into a renowned artist.

Josef Herman came from a Polish Jewish family and grew up in impoverished circumstances in Warsaw. His father and his uncle owned a shoe factory as young men, but his uncle had sold it behind his father's back and used the money to emigrate to the US. Josef's father had no option but to make the best of it and made a meagre living as a shoemaker. In later life, Josef did not have many positive memories of his father, who was short-tempered and prone to violent outbursts. Josef held him responsible for throwing Josef's sister against the sides of her cot; an incident that might have caused serious injury and was probably the cause of her deafness.

The family – Josef also had a brother – lived in a poor district of Warsaw, an area with high tenement buildings. They lived on the ground floor in a shop. Josef remembered that it was very gloomy: 'We lived in a shop, one room, narrow, and dark. Two paraffin lamps burnt all day and night, one on the wall over David's [his father] square workbench, and one on the far end over the white tiled kitchen where my mother spent most of her time.' His parents were always at work: his father at the workbench mending shoes, and his mother in the kitchen carrying out domestic work for the family but also, darning socks, ironing and doing laundry for payment.

Josef had a very different relationship with his mother from the one he had with his father. He described her as kind and open-minded; she took him out for little trips around Warsaw that he remembered fondly: 'But with Sarah [his mother] I walked the streets in pride. She was sensitive, she was subtle, she was gentle, she was rare.' The family's circumstances were that of many poor Polish Jewish families. The reason so many tried to move to Austria and Germany at the beginning of the 20th century and after the First World War was the hope of making a better living. However, in the case of the Herman family, it was only Josef who ever managed to leave Poland.

The cramped nature of the family flat was exacerbated by the addition of members of their extended family, including two aunts and his great grandmother, who were unable to afford any accommodation of their own. Josef's lifelong habit of getting up in the early hours of the morning, around 5 am, was probably formed during his childhood; it was the only time of the day which afforded him some privacy and quiet when he was growing up.

When only four years old, Josef was taught to read by a physician who had made it his mission to improve the health of the poorer members of Warsaw's population while living among them. He obviously recognised Josef's intellectual curiosity and tried to stimulate his desire for learning; however, Josef did not initially enjoy school. His school education was clearly very old-fashioned and he describes the years from age five to twelve in his autobiography as 'the dullest of my life.' At the end of his time at school, there was a new headmaster who employed better-trained teachers and also managed to provide free lunches with the help of an American charity. This improved things for Josef but, nevertheless, at the age of 13 he was taken out of school and told to get a job. Initially, Josef found it very hard to keep a position; it seems that often he lost jobs because he was not physically strong enough to carry them out. On one occasion, his boss at a cardboard box factory sacked him for collapsing in the street while out delivering a load of boxes. As a parting piece of advice, this employer suggested that Josef tell his mother to feed him more meat. Clearly, the family's poverty meant she would have been unable to comply. However, Josef was fortunate and a local Jewish man who worked in the printing industry and was heavily engaged in union work helped him to get an apprenticeship at a printer's as a machinist and typesetter.

This was a fortuitous opportunity for someone with a natural eye for aesthetics and composition. It also gave Josef the opportunity to join the typesetters' union, which had a programme of educational and cultural events. A supervisor recognised that Josef was capable of more creative tasks and supplied him with magazines on modern graphic art. This enabled him to take on graphic design tasks, an area he worked in for a number of years. He also joined a group of young men that made it their aim to reclaim the Yiddish language and culture. In his autobiography, Josef describes this as the moment when he became proud of his Jewish heritage. By the time that graphic design started to feel like a limited and routine task, he had friends who were able to introduce him to a group of writers and painters in Warsaw. First, Josef began to model for artists' life classes, and then he started painting himself having been told that you have to have an instinctive sense for pigment to be a painter. Josef sensed that he had this 'itch in [his] fingertips' and from now on pursued this path. From 1930 to 1932, he attended the Warsaw School of Art and Decoration and, in 1932, he had his first exhibition in a small gallery in Warsaw connected to a framing shop.

During the 1930s, the political situation in Poland was getting increasingly difficult. Poland was ruled by what amounted to a military dictatorship that tried to oppress both the Jewish population and left-wing activities in general. There were right-wing antisemitic groups attacking Jewish people and Jewish businesses. Along with many fellow students and artists, Josef was arrested several times. Most of the time he was released quickly, but on one occasion he was told by the Polish police that they did not need any proof of actual anti-government or left-wing activity to put him in prison for a long time.

In 1938, Josef decided to leave Poland and to emigrate to Belgium. Friends joined together to pay for his train fare and raised funds for his first few weeks in Belgium. He managed to get a short-term tourist visa for the country but hoped he would manage to arrange something more long-term after his arrival. It is clear that his friends and family saw the writing on the wall and realised that a young Jewish artist like Josef had no future in Poland. His mother is supposed to have told him at the train station to never come back, sensing the even more difficult times that were to come for Poland. She was right. She, his father, brother and sister, and almost all of his other relatives were murdered in the Holocaust.

Art historians have debated whether Josef would have been better off emigrating to Paris, but it has been argued that the earthiness of the art in Belgium was closer to his developing artistic style. However, with the benefit of hindsight, we know that neither Belgium nor France would ultimately offer any permanent form of sanctuary to a Polish Jew. When Belgium was invaded in May 1940, Josef fled to France. He was helped by an American woman with a car, getting away from the advancing German army with only the clothes on his back, including his black leather coat.

The next phase of his escape was as bizarre as it was lucky. On arriving at the port of Bordeaux, Josef overheard a group of Poles discussing a Greek ship at La Rochelle that was supposed to take Poles to Canada. He had no idea how he would get onto such as ship, but an American friend helped him reach La Rochelle. There, the Polish Military Police mistook him for a member of the Polish Airforce on account of his black leather coat. He was arrested for desertion and led, alongside thousands of Polish soldiers, onto the very ship he was searching for. However, this ship did not set sail to Canada but brought its Polish passengers to Britain. The British Home Office was not pleased by the arrival of unexpected refugees like Josef, but return was clearly impossible, and as the Polish Army was in Scotland and the Polish Consul in Glasgow, they sent him to live in Glasgow where he arrived in the summer of 1940.

In Glasgow, Josef met the sculptor Benno Schotz who told him that Josef's friend from Warsaw, Yankel Adler, was also living in the city. Adler was an artist with interests in many fields and many traditions, who had been a friend of the well-known German artist Paul Klee. Josef settled into the artists' community in Glasgow quickly, managing to find a studio and begin painting again soon after his arrival. In other respects, Josef's integration proved a little more difficult. He spoke Yiddish, Polish and French but no English. However, he took English lessons, and obviously learnt the language quickly. Josef started to exhibit within a year. His first exhibition was in 1941 at James Connell and Sons in Glasgow.

In 1942, the Red Cross informed Josef that his entire family, who had been living in the notorious Warsaw Ghetto, had been murdered. Throughout the war years – and even from concentration camps and ghettos – the International Red Cross managed to keep up some form of communication via letters and especially postcards, which were only allowed to contain 25 words or less. Josef suffered a breakdown on receiving the news about his family. His success as an artist continued, however. He exhibited in Edinburgh, and this exhibition attracted the attention of a fellow Scottish artist, Catriona MacLeod. After buying some of his works, she travelled to Glasgow to ask Josef whether he would take her on as a pupil. Josef declined, saying that he did not take on pupils but they obviously liked each other as they started a relationship and were married later the same year.

By this time, the name of Josef Herman had become well known to art critics and gallery owners. He moved to London and held his first solo exhibition at the Reid and Lefevre Gallery in King Street. Life in London during the war became increasingly difficult for the then pregnant Catriona, however, as she was unable to sleep because of the frequent air raids. The couple started to look for an escape, away from city life, and considered the Brecon Beacons in Wales. Unfortunately, when they stayed overnight in Brecon, it turned out to be noisy and full of soldiers and their girlfriends partying into the early hours.

The couple went looking for a quieter location and found one. Josef later said that they were both overwhelmed at their first sight of Ystradgynlais. They arrived on a hot June or July day and the village was quiet with hardly anyone to be seen. There was a bridge with a thin stream and the water and the pebbles glistened in the sun, Suddenly, a group of miners appeared, reminding Josef of religious imagery with their black bodies and what looked like shining haloes caused by the bright sunlight. After crossing the bridge, the miners dispersed and walked to their different homes in the village. The magnificence of the image stayed with Josef and he depicted these or similar groups of miners in many of his paintings. Initially, the couple rented the former top floor ballroom of the Pen-y-Bont Inn, which served them as both artist's studio and living quarters. There is a photograph taken there of Josef and Catriona having tea on an ironing board while sitting on the end of their bed.

Josef later described arriving in the village as the beginning of a new phase in his artistic development. He started charcoal and pastel drawings, and by 1946 he had made about a hundred pastel drawings, a number of which were selected for another exhibition in London. In 1946, he started painting in oil again and the couple bought a derelict lemonade factory and converted it into a studio and a home.

We know about Josef's time in Ystradgynlais from the posthumously published *Related Twilights: Notes from an Artist's*

Diary, which contains both autobiographical notes and drawings. He was taken both with the landscape and with the local people. He states that 'the miner' is the man of Ystradgynlais. The river Tawe is described as having always one colour more than the sky. He was fascinated by the local houses with doors that were smaller than the men.

Biographers and art critics have had a tendency to ask questions about Josef such as, 'What made this Polish Jewish refugee choose a small Welsh village for his base for over a decade?' and 'What made this painter choose Welsh miners, the local community and the Tawe (Cwm Tawe in Welsh) Valley landscape as his main subject matter from 1944 to 1955?' But these are the wrong questions. We know why Josef left Warsaw, why he fled Belgium and France, and how he ended up in the UK. Moving to new places is normal for many people just as staying in the same location is normal for others. Clearly Josef was very aware of this question and the need to give an explanation why he stayed in South Wales. In his *Notes from a Welsh Diary*, published in 1987, he claimed that Ystradgynlais had all he needed: 'I stayed on because here I found ALL I required. I arrived a stranger for a fortnight. The fortnight became eleven years.' There is no reason to doubt that this was the case. As we know, Josef and Catriona were looking for a quiet place. The sense of stability that could be achieved in a small community undoubtedly suited them. The landscape and the people inspired Josef and he was able to make a fresh start in his painting. In *Notes* he writes about his admiration of the figure of the miner and in a BBC Radio broadcast discussing South Wales he claimed that the miner was the archetypal working man. Such a perception was widespread internationally for much of Josef's life and it may be that part of his fascination with the miners was that they reminded him of a shared history of the working class across Europe. It has been claimed that the miners in Josef's paintings are monumental, both timeless and enduring. It is certainly the case that Josef's paintings communicate the strong sense of solidarity that has always been a feature in mining communities. The miners' reliance on and trust in one another while down the mine extended into their community life and leisure time. The community of Ystradgynlais was small and tight-knit, but at the same time the villagers were willing to admit and welcome Josef and his wife. "'You're no stranger here,' I was told the very day I arrived,' he recalled. 'A day later I was addressed as Joe, and soon I was nick-named Joe-bach.' The fact that mining is such a dangerous occupation probably helped their integration. The community was used to death and grief. For a man like Josef, who had lost his entire family in Poland, and suffered further grief when Catriona's pregnancy ended in a stillbirth not long after their arrival in the village, it was probably easier to live amongst the Welsh miners and their families, many of whom had seen tragedy as well. In *Notes*, Josef remarks on the ailing miners whose lungs had become poisoned by silica dust. He says it is remarkable how they bear their illness and how they downplay the seriousness of their condition: 'A bit short of breath,' they would say. But it is clear that in a similar vein, Josef continued his life after the murder of almost all his relatives because there was nothing else to do about it. The rawness in the paintings depicting the Welsh miners can be seen to reflect the raw grief of losing so many family members in the Holocaust. After so much loss, he drew consolation from the closeness of a tight-knit community.

Although Josef himself was from Warsaw, the villages in Wales were not so dissimilar from the villages in eastern Europe that were part of many refugees' memories. For example, in 1943, the British film-maker Humphrey Jennings shot a short film called *The Silent Village* on location in Cwmgiedd, just outside Ystradgynlais, to tell the story of the Nazi massacre of the Czech mining community of Lidice.

There are different takes on Josef's integration into the village. It has been claimed by others that Herman's integration was only superficial and that he did not mix much socially with the village community. Their closest friends were Dai Alex, a National Coal

Board Official and a poet, and Peggy Williams. Josef was also close to the photographer Llew Morgan. It's likely the couple – and their friends – would have raised an eyebrow or two with their bohemian and eccentric dress sense.

Josef and Catriona did not learn the Welsh language, although in *Notes* he called Welsh the only language that expressed the music of sorrow, certainly acknowledging its existence, distinctiveness, and beauty. Josef was made honorary chair of the Male Voice Choir during his time in Ystradgynlais. Whether or not Josef was well integrated into South Wales village life is clearly a matter for discussion or a matter of definition. Josef was a painter not a miner. However, there seems to have been a mutual respect between himself and his fellow villagers concerning the others' skill and hard work. As mentioned before, Josef would always get up very early in the morning. In *Notes from a Welsh Diary*, he wrote: 'At five each morning I hear hobnailed boots on the road. I go to the window of my room at the Pen-y-Bont Inn. Miners in the dark going to work. Some look up to my light and lift an arm up in greeting. When the echoes of the feet fade, I leave the window and go on with my work...'

The scene that conveys mutual respect and a certain degree of shared feeling. Apparently, many of his neighbours visited his exhibition in Swansea or would drop in for a chat at his studio.

The exhibition at Swansea's Glynn Vivian Art Gallery was the first time his work depicting the miners was exhibited in Wales. The gallery in Swansea was the first stop on a tour of ten locations for the exhibition entitled *Ystradgynlais: Paintings, Pastels and Drawings by Josef Herman*, which was organised by the Arts Council of Great Britain. The tour ended in Pontypool. Not all locations were traditional galleries, which must have suited Josef's political convictions. Although he was not as politically active as the photographer Edith Tudor-Hart, Josef also had left-wing sympathies and making the under-represented working class the subject of his paintings and exhibiting these paintings was important to him.

The post-war British government made it relatively easy for former refugees to apply for UK citizenship. Josef applied for naturalisation in 1948. Before then he had to travel on the papers of a 'stateless person' issued by the British government, which was obviously inconvenient and attracted unwanted attention from officials. But it seems likely that he was keen to become British for more than just the sake of convenience. He clearly felt at home in Wales, and he had lost all family connections in Poland.

In those days, a lot of the applicants for naturalisation were visited at home by Home Office officials. The official who visited Josef in Ystradgynlais noticed the books on his shelves and commented that Josef must be a man of the left. Josef later recalled that he replied in the affirmative and implied that surely every sensible individual was on the left, including the man from the Home Office. Josef remembers that his naturalisation papers came through immediately afterwards. This is a good anecdote if true, and in this case no negative consequences derived from Josef's audacity and honesty. There were cases, however, when naturalisation was denied on the grounds of left-wing convictions, the UK government being suspicious of left-wing activity, leaving the former refugee in stateless limbo for decades.

By the late 1940s, Josef Herman had become well known in Wales and beyond. One staunch advocate of his work was David Bell, Regional Officer of the Arts from 1946 and subsequently (from 1953) Assistant Director of the Welsh Arts Council. Josef was commissioned to produce a large mural for the Minerals of the Island Pavilion at the forthcoming Festival of Britain. Timed to mark 100 years since the Great Festival of 1851, the Festival of Britain was designed to celebrate national achievement after the end of the Second World War. It attempted to showcase life in the UK in its entirety with works of art bringing together the perspectives of different nations, different social classes and different backgrounds. In some way, Josef's monumental portrayal of the Welsh miners did just that. Painted by a Polish Jewish refugee, a naturalised British citizen, his art showed, according to critics, both the individualism of the miners and a more generalised monumentality. These particular paintings of miners have been compared to Ancient Egyptian paintings and called iconic. On a more sociological level, it was clearly not thought to be problematic to commission a Polish refugee from National Socialism to create a work of art depicting Welsh miners for a festival intended to celebrate Britain.

Herman's art clearly struck a chord with the post-war British public. Unfortunately, the original mural has not survived in its entirety as it had to be cut up during a studio fire in order to save at least some parts. Many of Herman's paintings and prints survive in Wales, including at Aberystwyth University's School of Art, and across the UK, including at the Tate gallery in London. Some of Josef's work was collected by the Davies sisters, Gwendoline and Margaret, who lived in mid-Wales. Their collection is considered as one of the great British, and certainly Welsh, art collections of the 20th century. They bequeathed 260 works to the National Museum of Wales after their deaths in 1951 and 1963. Critics argue that the Davies sisters' collection completely transformed the National Museum of Wales's art collection. Several works by Josef were part of their 19th and 20th century collection as were works by Cézanne and Pissarro, Oskar Kokoschka and Eric Gill.

Greater national attention took Josef away from Ystradgynlais frequently in the early 1950s. He left Wales in 1955, mainly for health reasons. Josef suffered from respiratory illness and was advised by his doctors to leave for a dryer climate. In 1955, Catriona and Josef divorced and Josef subsequently married Nini Ettlinger, a fellow refugee from National Socialism, who had been born in Berlin in 1935. The couple had two children, David and Rebeka.

Josef Herman had a long and productive life. He died in the year 2000 in West London but the core of his artistic legacy remains his paintings of the miners of Ystradgynlais.

41

Portrait of Edith Tudor-Hart, c. 1936 by Rudolf Bauer
(© the Estate of W. Suschitzky)

Demonstration, Trealaw, 1935 by Edith Tudor-Hart
(© the Estate of W. Suschitzky)

THE CAMERA AS WEAPON:
EDITH TUDOR-HART IN
THE RHONDDA VALLEY

Some refugees only spent a short time in Wales, but their legacy remains significant for Welsh history and culture. The photographer Edith Tudor-Hart is one of these. Edith lived in the Rhondda Valley with her husband Alex Tudor-Hart for a few months in 1934–5. Alex was a physician who tried to provide medical care for the working-class population of the area free of charge. This fitted in with the couple's communist political convictions; a political commitment that is reflected in the iconic photographs Edith took at the time. They depict striking miners, unemployed workers, and the terraced houses of the mining communities typical of both the era and area. Her life story is exciting and tragic, involving frequent moves between countries and places as is often typical for refugees from National Socialism. Like many others in this position, she constantly attempted to connect different communities and cultures through her photography.

Edith Tudor-Hart was born Edith Suschitzky into a Viennese Jewish family in 1908; her parents were social democrats. Her father owned a bookshop and later a small progressive publishing house in Vienna. From early childhood, she was used to meeting left-wing authors and intellectuals at home, discussing politics among an international circle of friends. The family greeted the Russian Revolution of 1917 enthusiastically. Edith soon outgrew her social democratic upbringing and joined the Communist Youth movement. Aged just 17, she first left Vienna for London in order to train as a Montessori Kindergarten teacher.

Progressive education, even for very young children, was seen as an important pillar supporting the fight for political change. There was a need to replace old-fashioned hierarchical schooling that aimed to produce citizens who unquestioningly followed those in authority. Working-class children, especially, would be encouraged to explore the world through play and discover their inner creativity. Many young left-wing women wanted to be part of this change in early years' education, which was both groundbreaking and somewhat conservative. It was mainly young women who were trained as nursery teachers, while their male counterparts entered other professions. In some ways this was typical of Edith's life story. She had the energy, creativity and conviction to facilitate change but it was often her position as a woman in a patriarchal world that held her back, in some instances with catastrophic consequences.

At the Montessori college in London where she trained from 1 April to 20 July 1925, Edith met Beatrix Tudor-Hart who was also a trainee teacher. Through Beatrix she met her brother, Alex. Both Beatrix and Alex were from an aristocratic background; the children of the painter Percyval Tudor-Hart, who had once shared a studio with Henri Toulouse-Lautrec in Paris. Both Beatrix and Alex were committed communists. Edith had already been part of the Communist Youth movement in Austria and was immediately attracted to Alex, who was studying medicine, despite him being eight years older and married. It seems that Alex and Edith had a brief, but very intense, relationship before she returned to her family in Vienna in the summer of 1925. We know that in Vienna she fell in love a second time with a man who was already in a relationship with another woman. Arnold Deutsch and his girlfriend, also a Montessori teacher, were both Jewish and members of the Austrian Communist Party. Having a girlfriend did not stop Deutsch conducting a passionate affair with Edith, which involved borrowing a flat from a wealthy friend for their assignations. When Deutsch's girlfriend found out, he ended his relationship with Edith, who was hugely upset and became very depressed. Her family was concerned and tried to find ways to help her overcome her mental distress. One of the solutions they came up with was to give Edith a camera, which is how she came to start taking pictures of people in the streets of Vienna.

After spending the summer of 1926 with Swedish family friends, Edith returned to London in early 1927, where she lived with her friend Beatrix Tudor-Hart. She applied to become a member of the Communist Party of Great Britain. She also probably started seeing Alex Tudor-Hart again before returning to Vienna in autumn 1927.

During the late 1920s, Edith seems to have been living between two countries and between two lovers. Eventually Arnold Deutsch and his girlfriend were ordered to move to Moscow by the Communist Party and Edith was again left upset in Vienna. This seemed to spur her on to develop her photography, and she took many more photographs in Vienna around that time. Her talent was clearly recognised by members of her family who also realised that she was still in a vulnerable emotional state. They seem to have come to the decision that she would benefit from leaving Vienna and maybe studying at university. Unfortunately, she had left school without the necessary qualifications so instead she went to study photography at the Bauhaus – the modernist art and design school founded in 1919 by the architect Walter Gropius – in Dessau in Germany, where a progressive outlook and artistic talent was seen as more important than the right school certificates.

Many leading members of the Bauhaus, such as Gropius and Mies van der Rohe, would later also have to flee National Socialist Germany. Gropius briefly lived in the UK, where he was supported by Jack Pritchard, the design entrepreneur responsible for building the Lawn Road Flats in Hampstead and other modernist developments. Pritchard also tried to help Edith with introductions after her final escape to London in 1933. Those few months of study at the Bauhaus in 1928 allowed Edith to explore the artistic zeitgeist of the time and hone her photographic art. The clear lines of her photographs remind us of the clear lines of Bauhaus architecture and design.

After Deutsch had left for Moscow, Edith clearly focused on her relationship with Alex Tudor-Hart. She remained in Britain, where she came to the attention of Scotland Yard. Edith had been a member of the British Communist Party since 1927. This in itself was not illegal but she was a foreigner with no permanent right of residency. When she was arrested at a demonstration in 1930, she was expelled from the UK and went back to Austria.

However, Austria in 1930 was no longer a welcoming place for a Jewish Communist. The First Austrian Republic had been founded after the end of the First World War, but as in Germany the newly established democratic system was too weak to withstand the constant onslaught of non-democratic, mainly right-wing, forces. Under threat from day to day, the Republic lasted until 1933, when Chancellor Engelbert Dollfuss ended parliamentary rule and established an autocratic regime, sometimes called Austrofascism. After that, it must have become abundantly clear to someone as politically astute as Edith that she had to get out of Austria fast. On 16 August 1933, Edith married Alex Tudor-Hart, who had divorced his first wife, at the British Embassy in Vienna. Their marriage allowed her to obtain a British passport a few days later, and the couple travelled to London immediately. They set up house in Brixton and Alex received money from his father to set up a GP's surgery.

Edith's escape came just in time as the political situation in Austria dramatically worsened. The Social Democrats and their paramilitary wing – the Schutzbund – were outlawed by the Dollfuss government in 1934, leading to civil war. In February 1934, several members of the Schutzbund were executed and many Social Democrats were imprisoned or had to flee. Edith's father, Wilhelm Suschitzky, who had suffered from depression intermittently for some time, could not cope with this deterioration of the political situation. Disillusioned with the end of the peaceful socialism he had believed in, Wilhelm took his own life in April 1934.

On 1 May 1934, the Austrofascists imposed a new constitution cementing Dollfuss's power. However, on 25 July 1934, during a right-wing power struggle, Dollfuss was assassinated as part of a coup attempt by the National Socialists and Kurt Schuschnigg became Chancellor of Austria. Schuschnigg kept Austria on a German-aligned course but wanted to keep it a separate country. During this time, Edith's mother and brother in Vienna faced an increasingly difficult situation both because of their political convictions, and because their left-leaning bookshop and publishing house was not allowed to operate without harassment.

Meanwhile in the UK, Edith and Alex were not only committed to their Communist goals in theory, they also wanted to help deprived working-class communities in practice. Hence, they moved to Llanelli so that Alex could provide free health care for local miners and their families. While Alex worked long hours in the surgery, Edith explored the area with her camera. She took pictures of the terraced houses in the Rhondda Valley; of a group of men at Monmouth Assizes; of unemployed workers in Abertillery, standing in front of a wall with the painted inscription 'All Roads lead to Monmouth jail'; of an unemployed workers' demonstration in Trealaw; and of two miners taking home pit props, as she calls them in the title of the photograph. One of her most famous pictures, *Demonstration in the Rhondda*, shows a huge march in the rain against the Unemployment Act of 1934. Most of her photographs depict working men, but there are also a smaller number showing working-class women in South Wales. One image – of an older woman – would later be used as the cover picture of a 1939 Penguin paperback entitled *Working-Class Wives* by Margery Spring Rice, which drew on first-hand accounts of their health and lives by ordinary women. More of Edith's pictures, from both London and Wales, are included inside the book.

When looking at Edith's photographs taken in the 1930s, it is striking how similar some of the photographs of the working class in the Rhondda Valley are to those she took in the East End of London and in Vienna: especially when depicting street protests.

Edith's work never objectifies her subjects. One of her most memorable photographs depicts a girl in torn clothes looking longingly into the window display of a cake shop. The message of the photograph is clear: hunger and inequality are painful. Yet, Edith's photograph also captures the girl's individuality. Her work is a testament to, and a commemoration of, an international working class, showing not only deprivation and poverty but also solidarity and community.

This is equally true of the photographs she took in Wales and England. Some of the photographs taken in the mining communities in the Rhondda Valley were published in *The Geographical Magazine* in March 1936 to accompany a report on the Rhondda Valley. The article discusses the British National Government's Special Areas Commission. The photography expert and curator Duncan Forbes rightly points out that these are not mere stock photos and that the photographed individuals were able to choose how they represented themselves. The photographs are taken from close proximity and we can sense the mutual dialogue between the photographer and the photographed.

Putting Edith's photographs of the demonstrations in 1930s Austria and the photographs of the striking workers in Wales side by side, it is easy to see the connections between the struggles of the working class in different parts of Europe such as Vienna and the Rhondda. Edith's work shows that Wales is not the marginal country with a quaint history that is sometimes depicted by Anglo-centric British history writers. Edith did not see Welsh miners as marginal and unimportant but as engaged in the resistance to capitalism and right-wing ideology. She represents their struggle as part of a pan-European political struggle. Her view as someone newly arrived in Wales helped her to see connections with a clearer eye and, as a photographer, with a clearer lens.

Not all critics respond entirely positively to Edith's work: some argue that her work is too directly responsive to what she saw and thus reveals too much of her anger with the societal conditions and political developments. One called her 'a photographer with vengeance'. Edith clearly had a lot to be angry about; however, she used her gift for photography to show the situation of the marginalised and documented their stories. In South Wales, she had the viewpoint of the recently arrived outsider, but managed to keep a dialogue going with the local community through her art. We are fortunate to have access to her work today, but in the first half of the 20th century she did not always have the opportunities she deserved to showcase that work. During the early 1940s, she placed photographs in the picture magazine *Lilliput*, which was edited by a fellow exile Stephan Lorant. Duncan Forbes, who is an expert on her photographic art, argued that she never managed to publish a definite testimony and her brother Wolf Suschitzky stated in an address he held on the occasion of a posthumous exhibition in 2013 in Vienna that this was the first exhibition that could be seen as his sister's 'monograph'.

Edith supported the workers' photography movement in the UK and the foundation of two workers' photography associations in the UK.

The Tudor-Harts moved back to London after a few months in Wales and Alex Tudor-Hart tried to establish himself as a GP in South London. We can assume this was for financial reasons as he needed to make a living. He did not find it easy to attract the necessary paying patients in London either, despite having received money from his father to establish his GP practice. The couple lived in Brixton and on 14 April 1936 their son Tommy Tudor-Hart was born. We can imagine that it was not easy for Edith to be tied down at home with a small infant, nor for Alex to run his practice with a baby in the house. In 1936, Alex decided to go and support the Republican cause in the Spanish Civil War and work as a surgeon. Edith was not best pleased with this plan, and Alex seems to have left her without any financial support and without considering how she would manage as a single mother with a baby. Initially he had promised to only stay for three months, but he didn't return to

Britain for over two years, having hardly communicated with his wife during this absence. An additional difficulty was that Tommy seemed to have been neurodivergent, or possibly suffered from a condition that has been variously described as autism or schizophrenia. Neither condition would have been easy to diagnose at a young age and especially in the 1930s, but would almost certainly have made Tommy a difficult child to care for.

Edith ran out of money quickly and had to sell the house in Brixton, which Alex bitterly criticised her for on his return. She tried to make a living as a photographer both by working in photographic studios and selling her work to magazines, but this proved – unsurprisingly – very difficult.

Political developments at home in Austria can only have exacerbated Edith's unhappy situation. Under pressure from Austrian and German National Socialists, Dollfuss announced a referendum on the question of whether Austria should become part of Germany or stay independent on 9 March 1938, with the referendum taking place four days later on 13 March. However, on 12 March National Socialist Germany annexed Austria and Hitler made a triumphant entry into Vienna and spoke on the Heldenplatz in the centre of the city. Photographs of the time show thousands and thousands of Austrians cheering and welcoming this development.

The Anschluss, as the annexation of Austria by Germany was referred to, made many Austrian Jews and opponents of National Socialism realise that they would have to flee Austria, or the Ostmark, as it was now known, as soon as possible. Edith managed to facilitate her mother's escape, possibly by helping her get a domestic permit, i.e. a visa that allowed her to live and work in the UK as a domestic servant. Edith's brother Wolf fled to the UK a few months later on a Kindertransport.

Alex Tudor-Hart returned to the UK from Spain in early 1939. While he no doubt used his medical skills in the British Medical Unit to save lives, he was highly traumatised by what he had seen.

The pressure of work had been so overwhelming that he often just slept on the operating table in between operations. He was haunted by the stress of the experience and found it hard to sleep even after his return to London. He abused alcohol and was physically violent towards Edith. Once the Second World War started, he abandoned his family for a second time and disappeared for a number of months, taking up positions in hospitals and living away without informing his wife or ensuring support for his son. The couple eventually separated. Tommy's special needs were also becoming more and more apparent. For some months, Tommy saw the psychoanalyst Anna Freud – herself an exile from Austria who had come to England with her father Sigmund – for therapeutic sessions as he also had trouble sleeping and settling at school. Unfortunately, even after therapy there was no improvement. Living through the nightly bombings in London also made things worse for him.

Eventually a place was found for him in a Camphill Community in Scotland, possibly in one of the first communities founded in Aberdeenshire in 1939. The Camphill Communities were based on Rudolf Steiner's spiritual philosophy of 'anthroposophy', the belief that each human being has a perfectly formed spirit independent of possible disabilities or mental health problems. The Camphill Movement was founded by fellow refugee and Austrian paediatrician Karl König and is based on the principles of anthroposophy. König believed every human being possessed a healthy inner personality that was independent of their disability. The role of the Camphill Community and school was to nurture and educate this essential self. It is easy to see that these circumstances would have inspired confidence in Edith that such an environment would meet Tommy's complex needs and offered a holistic way for him to lead a full life.

It has been suggested that Tommy Tudor-Hart's difficulties – his possible schizophrenia – might have been caused by his mother's clandestine political activities. From a 21st century point of view, this seems unlikely, especially as we have no proof as to the exact nature of his special needs. Nor do we know much about the exact nature of Edith's activities and how they might have impacted her day-to-day life. However, we do know that she was a Communist, moved in Communist circles, and had some connections to the Comintern, the international organisation promoting World Communism. Her former lover Arnold Deutsch and her love rival Josefine had been recruited by the Comintern's International Liaison Department, probably when they were in Moscow. By the mid-1930s, however, Arnold was living in London in one of the Lawn Road Flats and back in touch with Edith. While Edith had been depressed by Deutsch's departure from Vienna, she had remained close to him and it is speculated that she was the person who suggested to him the recruitment potential of idealistic young students from upper middle-class backgrounds to spy for the Soviet Union. These students would be encouraged to denounce their Communist sympathies and upon graduation they would have easy access to careers in the civil service or the government. Deutsch recruited Kim Philby in July 1934. He trained and advised him, and became his handler. Later in 1934, Deutsch also recruited Donald Maclean and Guy Burgess, who would all be seen later as members of what came to be known as the Cambridge Five. None of the known members of this infamous spy ring were ever prosecuted, although Burgess, Maclean and, later, Philby were all forced to flee to the Soviet Union.

Edith's biographer and nephew Peter Stephan Jungk has unearthed some evidence of her political activities though the full extent of her involvement is unknown. Any files that might be in existence in the archives of the KGB in today's Russia either do not exist any more or are locked away still. Edith's activities may never have extended much beyond being a Communist Party member and a courier and probably never warranted her arrest or a trial. However, on 8 January 1952 – at a time when it was first alleged that Philby had warned Burgess and Maclean that they were suspected of being spies – she was visited by MI5 officials who threatened her and warned her to stop any clandestine activity. They made it clear that taking photographs in any shape or form could be seen as proof of her espionage activity. Reports by the two officials who questioned Edith exist and have been examined by Peter Stephan Jungk. After this visit and interview, Edith's mental health became fragile. She ended up spending three months in West Park Hospital in Epsom. It has been suggested that her admission to this psychiatric hospital was actually engineered by her Russian spymaster as a way to remove her from the public eye in London.

What happened in early 1952 led Edith to destroy the back catalogue in her studio and a lot of her photographic negatives. It spelled the end of her career as a photographer. Edith lost the weapon she had used so effectively against the oppression of the working class and injustice. It seems that after this she was a broken woman. After her release from hospital, she moved to a new flat in London, near Hampstead Heath, and started working as a sales assistant at the Heal & Son store in Tottenham Court Road. She also broke with most of her old friends and only saw her brother Wolf and his wife Ilona occasionally.

Eventually, Edith moved to Brighton and ran a small antique business in Bond Street, living in a tiny flat above the shop. She shared the flat with her mother Alice until the latter moved to a care home. It is not difficult to imagine Edith as a successful antique dealer with her eye for style and composition. But it was a long way from her attempts to change the world through her political actions and her photographic work. She died in Brighton in 1973.

The photographic work that was not destroyed is today held in the National Galleries of Scotland and the National Portrait Gallery, amongst others, including the photographs taken in Wales. In 2013, a retrospective show was organised in the city of her birth, Vienna. Her brother Wolf travelled to Vienna for the opening. It can be seen as a sort of homecoming or rehabilitation for Edith Suschitzky in the city that had shaped her and her photographic art but then rejected her. From December 2019 to March 2020, three of her photographs, including *Demonstration in the Rhondda*, were displayed in the Refuge and Renewal: Migration and British Art exhibition, first shown at the Royal West of England Academy in Bristol. The exhibition was then due to move to the Museum of Modern Art in Wales, in Machynlleth. Sadly, the Covid 19 pandemic denied this particular homecoming to Wales. However, the fact that her photographs depicting South Wales were included in such an exhibition speak to their long-lasting significance.

Edith Tudor-Hart was a modern woman and her documentary photographic work comprised a modernist project. However, due to the takeover of National Socialism and Fascism in Europe, and due to her position as a woman, suffering domestic and emotional abuse, her ambitions and potential were thwarted. Her photographic legacy remains to remind us of a time when an international working-class movement extended from Vienna to the valleys of South Wales.

South Wales, c.1934 by Edith Tudor-Hart
(© the Estate of W. Suschitzky)

Terraces, South Wales, c.1935 by Edith Tudor Hart
(© the Estate of W. Suschitzky)

Dolli, Käthe & Kate Bosse, 1913 (© Heini Gruffudd)

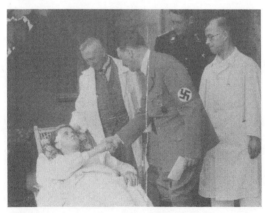

Paul Bosse with Hitler while he was chief surgeon at the
Paul-Gerhard Stift, Wittenberg, 1935 (© Heini Gruffudd)

THE WELSH LANGUAGE AND CULTURE AS AN ACT OF RESISTANCE: KATE BOSSE-GRIFFITHS AND CYLCH CADWGAN

Kate (Käthe) Bosse was born in 1910 and grew up in a relatively privileged family in Wittenberg in Germany but, as we will see, despite her father Paul's best efforts, this did not help the family evade the murderous aims of the Nazis. What makes Kate's story especially interesting is her subsequent complete immersion within the culture of Wales and the Welsh language. She left Germany for Britain in 1937 and, after marrying J. Gwyn Griffiths, moved to Wales in 1939 and never left. Kate's sons, Robat Gruffudd and Heini Gruffudd, continue to play an important part in Welsh cultural life, as writers, teachers and publishers.

Kate was persecuted as Jewish according to the Nuremburg Race Laws of 1935. In her case, this had nothing to do with her religious affiliation or any form of self-identification. Kate had been brought up as a Lutheran Protestant. But both Kate's maternal grandparents were Jewish, although they both had converted to Christianity. This meant that Kate's mother, also called Käthe, was considered Jewish, despite the fact that she had been raised from birth as a member of the Lutheran Church. Having two Jewish grandparents but not being part of the Jewish religious community herself meant that Kate was considered a *Mischling ersten Grades* – a 'mongrel of the first degree' – according to the warped Nazi ideology.

The fact that Kate's father, Paul Bosse, was not Jewish, but defined as 'Aryan', and came from a well-established Christian family in Wittenberg in Eastern Germany, where the founder of the Protestant reformation, Martin Luther, had lived and worked in the 15th and 16th century, made her family's experience different from the experience of families where all members were considered Jewish. Paul Bosse was a surgeon and held the position of clinical lead at the local hospital, the Paul-Gerhardt-Stift, which was affiliated to the Lutheran church. Paul was revered in Wittenberg and beyond, as a surgeon and as an obstetrician. He had also served in the First World War as a medical officer and had been severely wounded. Even under the Nazis, and even initially for Jews, having seen active service in the First World War afforded men some privileges, and exempted them from certain discriminatory policies, such as for example, the policy to terminate their employment as civil servants.

As a non-Jew, Paul had a different relationship to the Nazi regime, even though he was by no means supportive of their ideology, than a Jewish doctor would have done. He became an accredited physician for the German sprinting team at the 1936 Olympic Games in Berlin, where Hitler tried to show the world the superiority of the new Germany and his Aryan master race (unsuccessfully in the case of the track sprints as the 100 metre and 200 metre races were both won by the black American athlete Jesse Owen).

The family was wealthy, owned a large house in Wittenberg and later several other properties and land. Kate and her siblings, Dolly, Günther and Fritz, were all afforded an excellent education. Kate, born in 1910, and her sister Dolly, born in 1907, were the only girls who were allowed to attend a local boys' grammar school. After successfully passing the German leaving certificate – the *Abitur* – Dolly went on to study medicine and Kate read Classics and Egyptology.

After the Nazi takeover in 1933, members of the Bosse family started to experience persecution because of their Jewish background. Fritz, born in 1915 and youngest brother of Kate, was not allowed to study at university because he was considered Jewish. His father bought him a farm instead, and Fritz started growing food and developing farm machinery. Despite not being Jewish himself, Paul Bosse started to experience discrimination and exclusion because he was married to a Jewish woman. Non-Jewish husbands and wives were encouraged to divorce their Jewish partners: some did so because they wanted to end the relationship, others divorced but tried to carry on with their relationship in secret, and some refused as did Paul Bosse. Having a non-Jewish spouse afforded the Jewish partner a certain degree of protection from the worst excesses of the Nazi persecution, at least during the early years of the regime. One famous example of a 'mixed marriage' was the case of the scholar and linguist Victor Klemperer who wrote on the language of National Socialism and also kept a diary chronicling the never-ending restrictions and harassments in the everyday life of a Jew and his non-Jewish partner during the Third Reich. The diary was published posthumously to great acclaim in 1995. Klemperer's wife Eva refused to divorce him and eventually they were forced to live in a *Judenhaus*, accommodation just for Jews. Despite being continuously harassed by the Hitler Youth and questioned by the Gestapo, the secret police of Nazi Germany, Klemperer and his wife survived the war.

The attack on the private and professional life of the Bosse family started soon after January 1933. Some was due to pressure with not much legal basis, some was due to actual changes in the law. The murderous machine of National Socialism and the chaos that clearly reigned by the mid-1940s sometimes makes us forget that in the beginning the rule of law was not completely abandoned in Germany, but only slowly eroded. In 1933, a local prominent member of the SS, who was also a physician, tried to get Paul removed from his post as clinical lead at the hospital. One can only wonder about the motivation for such an attempt, but it likely included professional jealousy as well as ideology. Prominent members of the SS were unfortunately also well connected in the Lutheran Church, which ran the hospital, which made things more difficult. This attempt was, however, unsuccessful as Paul had plenty of supporters, and was a very able surgeon. In 1934, Dolly also narrowly escaped a ban on her practicing medicine. After the passing of the Nuremberg Race Laws in 1935, her situation was assessed a second time, but she again evaded being excluded from the medical register. It was argued that her application to join the medical council predated the 1935 rule that non-Aryans could not join. Clearly, there were still influential physicians in post who were not Nazis. Four years later, in 1938, Paul and Käthe's oldest son Günther was refused permission to practise medicine, while his sister Dolly managed to remain a doctor until she left Germany (it's not clear exactly when this was). Once again, it was argued successfully that she was exempt as she had been admitted to the German medical register in 1934. Günther who was younger and applied to get on the register later, was refused and was not allowed to be registered as a doctor and only worked as a medical assistant in his father's private clinic. This complex situation epitomises the position of a family that was well-established professionally and in the community, where not all members were considered Jewish but which nonetheless suffered many restrictions and much harassment.

Paul tried to use his position and his skills to protect his wife and children from Nazi policies. When an accident at a local explosives factory in 1935 resulted in around 100 deaths and 700 injured workers, it received press attention in Germany and internationally. It was even reported in *Time* magazine in the US. Paul led the care for the injured workers and used innovative medical techniques to treat them at the hospital in Wittenberg. Against initial expectations, almost all of the victims survived despite their serious injuries. Adolf Hitler himself visited the hospital: there is a photograph of Hitler shaking hands with one of the patients with Paul in the background. When Paul was asked by Hitler whether he wished anything as a reward for his exceptional work, he asked for his family to be spared repressions due to their Jewish background. Apparently, reassurances were given to him, though they proved to be false. Only months later, in December 1935, Paul was dismissed from his position as the lead doctor at the hospital.

Paul wrote to Goebbels to protest his dismissal, arguing that he had been assured that nothing bad would befall him and his family. In the letter he pointed out his 28 years of exemplary medical work at the hospital and referred to his active service in the First World War. He even signed the letter 'Heil Hitler' but no answer was received.

After his dismissal, Paul established a private hospital, incorporating maternity facilities, at his home by building an extension; it opened for patients in 1936. This private hospital in Wittenberg seems to have been very successful and Paul continued to be well-liked in the community. There were attempts to prevent the hospital from receiving sickness insurance funds but after a lengthy adjudication it was decided that Paul and his daughter Dolly were not 'Jewish' doctors as defined by Nazi race law and could therefore be members of the sickness insurance scheme. However, one condition was imposed on the family and the private hospital: Paul's wife Käthe was neither allowed to work in the clinic nor live there. This was of course difficult, as the clinic had been established in the Bosse family's private home. Kate's son, and her biographer, Heini Gruffudd describes how Kate's mother Käthe unsurprisingly felt very depressed, and it is reported that she felt responsible for the difficulties of the family, leading to suicidal thoughts. The best way that the family could find of sticking together and making the best of this difficult situation was for Käthe to live on her son Fritz's farm.

Daughter Kate was a modern, ambitious young woman. As well as studying Classics and Egyptology in Munich, Kate studied in Berlin and Bonn. She wrote her doctoral thesis on 'Human Figures in the Sculptures of the late Egyptian Period' and published this work in 1936. Kate's parents provided the financial backing for her studies and she was able to spend time in the museums in Berlin and Italy, as well as Greece and Egypt. At the time, Kate had a boyfriend who was also a student at Munich University. He helped Kate with drawings for her work, and she seems to have helped him with his studies. The boyfriend was clearly less successful than Kate.

When they became engaged, Kate's father was not keen as he did not think the fiancé would ever achieve much. Eventually the engagement was broken off. On 7 September 1935, Kate started working in the Egyptology department of the New Museum in Berlin, a state institution. However, she was dismissed on 9 May 1936, after a colleague pointed out to the head of the department that Kate was Jewish, because by then Jews were not allowed to be employed in public institutions. Her dismissal brought home the knowledge to Kate and her parents that she was not going to be able to have a professional career in Germany.

Her mother, Käthe, who was proficient in English, had visited England in younger years, and still had connections and friends in the country. She corresponded with the well-known zoologist and classicist, Sir D'Arcy Thompson, who was professor at St Andrews. He agreed to employ Kate as a secretary, and this clearly helped her gain a visa allowing her to enter and work in Britain. Kate arrived in the UK on 15 January 1937. She found St Andrews charming but also a little bit eccentric. The secretarial work for Thompson was not full-time, and likely not very interesting for someone with Kate's education, so she soon moved to London. Initially, she was refused permission to work as an au pair for a teacher in Brighton and to give German lessons at a private school. Instead, she was asked to make another application for leave to remain. At the same time, she tried to get a visa for the United States. A sympathetic academic based at the University of Chicago had written to many American institutions and museums praising Kate's scholarship. Most answers were not hopeful that they would be able to offer work to Kate as no US institution seemed to have an opening for a young Egyptologist.

In the UK, the Society for the Protection of Science and Learning (SPSL) was the major force behind finding employment for refugee academics. Eventually this organisation was able to help Kate find a temporary, part-time position at University College London, working in its Petrie Museum of Egyptian Archaeology.

Through the SPSL she made her first Welsh connection. The wife of Sir Clough Williams-Ellis of Portmeirion was a committee member.

Kate's move to Britain in 1937 was different from the desperate flight that some German Jews undertook only a couple of years later. Nonetheless, it was not a voluntary move but forced on her due to the fact that she was prohibited from working in her chosen profession in the country of her birth due to her Jewish ancestry. She remained in regular contact with her family in Germany and in September 1937 her parents even came to London to visit her; an occasion that was very much enjoyed by all. Kate visited Germany for one last time before the outbreak of war for Christmas 1937.

With hindsight, it seems strange that Paul and Käthe were still travelling throughout Europe in this way as late as September 1937, rather than attempting to leave Germany for good. In fact, the correspondence between Kate and her parents reveals that the whole family were discussing plans for emigration. However, no easy solution presented itself. One must also assume that Paul and Käthe were not willing to leave their established life in Wittenberg behind without some assurances that they would be able to establish a reasonable alternative outside Germany. In the summer of 1939, Kate saw her father for the last time in the Netherlands. By this time, her mother, Käthe, was no longer easily able to travel outside Germany.

In January 1939, Kate received an offer from Somerville College Oxford of a research grant for a project at the Ashmolean Museum where a new Egyptology exhibition had just opened. This was clearly not an opportunity to miss. The offer included a room at the college and dining rights, which meant that she could take her meals at the High Table with the other academics. There she met a scholar from Queen's College, J. Gwyn Griffiths, also a classicist with an interest in Egyptology, the son of a Baptist minister from Pentre, Rhondda. This meeting would change Kate's life.

The two academics immediately liked each other, and Gwyn spent a lot of time at the Ashmolean Museum. Gwyn was a Welsh speaker and an early member of Plaid Cymru. Plaid Cymru had been founded as Plaid Genedlaethol Cymru, the National Party of Wales in 1925 and had attracted members from a relatively broad political spectrum who felt that the promotion of the Welsh language and the political independence of the Welsh nation was of the utmost importance. Gwyn was on the left and pacifist side of the party.

Besides having been engaged years earlier in Germany, Kate had had other relationships with men, including at least one complicated one with a married man. Kate was very pragmatic about her position as a woman with regards to marriage and establishing a family. She discussed these issues in her letters. On the one hand, she wanted to have a family and children. On the other hand, she realised that any sort of relationship, not to mention becoming a mother, would restrict her freedom and make it more difficult for her to pursue her scholarly ambitions. All these considerations were also bound up with the fact that she had had to leave Germany and did not feel entirely at home in the UK. In a letter dated 4 April 1938, she writes: 'What do you want? *Have roots.* Where would you like to be? *In Germany.* Why don't you return? *Because I am not allowed to be in Germany during war.* [...] What remains for you, therefore? *Face reality.* 1) *woman ambassador* 2) *secretary* 3) *marry a man with whom you can have children.* You still have time for number 3. You're afraid to loose your ideal.'

Early in 1939, she had obviously finished weighing up the pros and cons of the situation and concluded that she did want to get married and have a family. When Gwyn left Oxford, the couple started writing to each other almost daily. They wrote in English but Gwyn gradually introduced Welsh words and provided grammatical explanations. Kate also introduced some German. Kate's letters reveal that she was keen to learn about Wales, and the Rhondda in particular, as well as the Welsh language. They also discussed their academic research and, of course, personal matters. Gwyn was in the process of applying for university positions, but was initially unsuccessful. They saw each other briefly when Kate stopped off in London in August 1939 on the way for that last meeting with her father in Holland.

In the second half of August, Kate returned to the UK but Gwyn had returned to his parents' house in Pentre. This made meeting up difficult, as there was no room in his parents' home for a guest. However, Kate did travel to Wales and took lodgings in Betws-y-Coed. While this was no more convenient for Pentre than England, she was able to explore the books in Welsh available there and Gwyn sent her some Welsh primers. In their correspondence, the couple discussed the impending war frequently. Gwyn considered all European powers as imperialistic oppressors and his position was that of a Welsh nationalist unwilling to fight on the side of the English oppressor. Unsuccessful in obtaining an academic post, he accepted a position as a schoolteacher at Porth County School, Rhondda.

When the Second World War broke out, Kate and Gwyn married quickly and secretly on 13 September 1939, only informing their families after the event. Gwyn's parents were accepting, and the couple lived with them initially while Gwyn worked as a schoolteacher. Soon the couple found a home of their own, not far away from Gwyn's parents. There they offered hospitality to many friends, including Pennar Davies – Gwyn's best friend – who would later become an influential Welsh writer and thinker. Kate learnt Welsh quickly, and not just for everyday life purposes: she wrote poems in German which she would then translate into Welsh, with Gwyn's help. In December 1940, a newly founded Welsh literary magazine *Heddiw* published a sonnet by Kate in Welsh entitled 'Moel Cadwgan'. She also wrote short stories to be published in Welsh, and these received considerable public attention. Kate enjoyed the rich Welsh-language cultural life of the Rhondda and she frequently compared the practices and the debates she encountered there with the traditions of ancient Greece and Rome.

Kate's willingness to immerse herself in the Welsh language and culture and her husband's background and ambition meant that the couple, but especially Kate, unintentionally became the centre of what might have been called a literary salon in the continental Europe of her upbringing, or a writers' group in today's terminology. They called this grouping Cylch Cadwgan, Cadwgan being the name of the mountain looming above their house. At its centre were Kate and Gwyn, and Pennar Davies, as well as the poet Rhydwen Williams. But there were numerous other influential Welsh writers, teachers, and thinkers who participated in the network, including many women. They had discussions about literature, philosophy and theology, including open discussions about sex, and the relationship between the genders. They read the work of well-known authors; for example, Kate guided them through Goethe's *Faust* and Dante's *Inferno*. But equally, if not more importantly, they also discussed and critiqued each others' writing.

They published their work in a wide range of formats: from the Welsh Baptists' paper *Seren Cymru* to literary magazines such as *Tir Newydd*. Heini Gruffudd, the couple's son, argues that Cylch Cadwgan formed a refuge of the mind for Welsh pacifists. Gwyn had in fact become a conscientious objector, and his arguments – prepared with Pennar Davies' help – were accepted and thus he did not have to join the British army.

Despite this rich cultural background of literature and thought, the early 1940s must have been very difficult years for Kate. She became pregnant with the couple's first child in 1940, but the baby was stillborn in 1941 suffering from hydrocephalus. Communication with her family was very difficult, as letters sent via the Red Cross took a long time in transit and frequently went undelivered. Occasionally, news was exchanged via friends and relatives abroad but no communication method was reliable.

Living in Wales, Kate clearly decided that one way to distance herself from the painful events on the continent was by continued immersion within the language and culture of Wales, which had become her home. In 1942, she won a short story competition run in the National Eisteddfod in Cardigan with her story 'Y Bennod Olaf', which was about a dying 18-year-old. The adjudicator of the competition specifically acknowledged Kate's ability to write about the modern world. This news reached the editor of *Die Zeitung*, an exile publication in London produced by German-speaking refugees for German-speaking refugees, and he asked for a German or English version of the story as he was unable to read the Welsh original.

Kate gave birth for a second time, in 1943, to Robat, who would later establish the Welsh publishing house Y Lolfa. After his birth, she started keeping her diary in Welsh – her adoption of the new culture and language had been fully completed.

For Kate, speaking Welsh and being Welsh embodied her anti-establishment attitude. The fact that such a stance was possible, and that her husband and many friends and supporters shared this stance, allowed her to inhabit an alternative cultural space, opposed both to English domination of Wales and to what had happened in Germany. In Nazi Germany protest had not been possible, and the ultimate triumph of the doctrine of National Socialism and the National Socialist state had forced Kate to leave her homeland. Adopting a new culture could be seen in part as an act of retrospective resistance to National Socialism. When Kate wrote, in Welsh, a pamphlet on pacifism in 1943, she was praised by Gwynfor Evans, who would become the leader of Plaid Cymru in 1945. Other small acts of resistance followed in later life, such as the refusal to pay for a parking ticket that was issued only in the English language, rather than bilingually or in Welsh.

Her first novel, *Anesmwyth Hoen* (Uneasy Joy), was published in 1941. It focuses on Welsh women's lives, but the narrative includes discussions of formerly taboo subjects such as sex outside marriage and abortion, which were franker than was customary in Welsh writing at the time. In some ways, it was closer in subject matter to some of the modern feminist novels published in Germany before National Socialism made such endeavours impossible and dangerous. Pushing against the boundaries of tradition, Kate received both praise and criticism for her work. In her short story collection *Fy Chwaer Efa* (My Sister Eva), first published in 1944, the stories focus on women's religious experience and mysticism as opposed to organised religion and so-called Western civilisation. Her second novel, *Mae'r Galon wrth y Llyw* (The Heart is at the Helm), came out in 1952 and was republished by Clasuron Honno in 2016. In this work, Kate again discusses the taboo subjects of love and sex outside marriage, and abortion, but also the position of women in society and the sacrifices they often have to make.

In the 1950s, Gwyn was appointed Professor of Classics at Swansea University College and the whole family moved to Swansea. Kate remained committed to the advancement of the Welsh language and joined protests against the dominance of English, notably refusing an English language parking notice. In Swansea, she returned to her earlier scholarly work and her academic training. She had been appointed to a post as Honorary Curator of Archaeology at Swansea Museum in 1949, and this position became even more exciting and significant when the British Museum offered more than 3,000 Egyptian artefacts from their Wellcome Collection to Swansea University College in 1971. Kate organised and catalogued the whole collection of Egyptian artefacts, which was made accessible to visitors through her labour. All her labels were bilingual in English and Welsh. Swansea Museum and later Swansea University, where the collection was eventually housed, were lucky to have the services of such an educated, skilled and dedicated curator. (The fact that she was not adequately remunerated is a rather shameful aspect of this arrangement.) Kate also wrote about the collection, both in scholarly journals and publications aimed at the general public. It seems that she enjoyed meeting visitors and passing on her knowledge of Egyptology and Archaeology face to face. There is photographic evidence of her interaction with museum visitors. This is another way in which Kate contributed to the culture and the public good in Wales, and there is a plaque in the museum to honour her contribution.

However, all of Kate's successes were achieved despite what had happened to her family left behind in Nazi Germany. After that final meeting with Kate in August 1939, the Bosse family's situation in Wittenberg became more and more difficult. There were minor changes in regulations that had a big impact on the ground: the Bosses were forced to get rid of their car, as non-Aryans were not allowed to drive and hence Paul could not visit his patients at home anymore. Attempts were made to find evidence against Paul in order to destroy the reputation of his private clinic. The Gestapo even set up an observation point from a neighbouring house to identify any possible infringements against rules governing the precarious situations of those married to Jews or considered 'mixed race'. It was a common tactic, and in line with National Socialist ideology to somehow link sexual issues considered taboo or 'dirty' with those not considered of 'pure Aryan race'. In this case, Paul was accused of infecting his female patients with sexually transmitted diseases. All protests to the national and local Nazi authorities against this sort of harassment were in vain, though it is interesting that the family still thought it actually worthwhile to write letters of complaint decrying their harassment and persecution.

On 20 July 1944, a group of army officers led by Claus von Stauffenberg made an assassination attempt on Hitler. The attempt failed but triggered the Nazi government into launching a wave of arrests targeting those considered in any way oppositional or racially inferior. Arresting, torturing and murdering unconnected individuals as an act of revenge for any perceived slight had been a Nazi tactic from the beginning of the regime. Paul and Käthe, their oldest daughter Dolly and her husband Georg, and the oldest Bosse son, Guenther, were all arrested and taken to the Gestapo prison in Wittenberg. Georg was released the next day but first ordered to undertake physical labour, then sent to the front as a doctor. Dolly was held without charge for six weeks and then released on the condition that she stay in Wittenberg and give up working as a doctor. Instead, she was forced to be a ground-digger at a soap factory. Fearing that her body would not be able to withstand the hardship and starvation, she escaped to hide with her three children in the West German town of Bad Wimpfen, where they owned a property. Paul spent nine weeks in prison without charge. Upon release, he was ordered to undertake physical labour for the Organisation Todt, a Nazi organisation that was notorious for using forced labour for its infrastructure projects. Fortunately, he was allowed to work as a doctor to treat foreign labourers within the Todt. He was again advised to divorce his wife, and again he refused.

Considered a Jew by dint of her parentage, Käthe's fate was worse than that of the others in her family. She was moved from the prison in Wittenberg to a prison in Halle, then onto Leipzig before being put on a transport to Ravensbrück concentration camp on 1 November 1944. Obviously, little is known of the details of what happened to Käthe in the camp. Ravensbrück was the largest concentration camp for women in the German Reich. Between its foundation in 1939 and its liberation by the Soviet Army at the end of April 1945 over 100,000 women were incarcerated there. It was a labour camp where women were exploited and violently treated and made to work in various industries including the armaments industry. By the end of 1944, the camp was very overcrowded and the sanitary conditions were catastrophic. Some women were housed in a tent, they had no blankets or other protection, and there were no toilets. By 16 December 1944, Käthe Bosse was dead. In February 1945, the family received a letter informing them that she had been sick and that despite the best efforts to treat her, she had died. The family even received 'her' ashes. Anyone studying the history of National Socialist Germany and the Holocaust knows that there was absolutely no truth in the content of such letters. It is also difficult to imagine that the ashes sent to the family were actually Käthe's ashes. But despite its murderous persecution of its Jewish citizens and of other Jews in Central Europe, as well of other groups of people it deemed undesirable, somehow the National Socialist state saw it fit 'to keep up appearances' and send letters of condolences as if they had not been entirely responsible for what happened.

Having a loyal husband and a certain standing in the local community, protected Käthe Bosse for some time from the worst of the National Socialist killing operation. Tragically, the liberation of the camps and the end of the war did not come quickly enough to save her. It is difficult to imagine how other family members coped with what had happened. Kate sent desperate telegrams to Germany, and for a while was of the erroneous belief that her brothers had also died. After May 1945, the new authorities in Wittenberg asked for Paul to return as a physician and tried to rehabilitate his reputation. However, they did not offer him his job as clinical lead of the whole hospital back, just the position as senior doctor of the part that was housed in his own family home. After his arrest, the Paul-Gerhard Stuft, his former employer, had simply taken over the Bosse home and requisitioned their consulting rooms and equipment. Asking him to come back to this was in some ways the ultimate insult. However, Paul was devastated to have lost his wife and working in the hospital was clearly the only way to carry on living. In December 1946, Paul suffered a heart attack. He died in March 1947 before Kate, who had only recently given birth to her second son, Heini, was able to see him again. It was only later that she managed to reunite with some of her family.

Kate found refuge in Wales and made it her permanent home. Her fight for the Welsh language and her creative writing in Welsh, as well as her work as a museum curator made an indelible mark on her new home country. Her sons continued with this work. In 2022, her son Robat Gruffudd and his wife Enid were chosen to lead the St. David's Day parade in Aberystwyth in an acknowledgement of their contribution to Welsh-language publishing. The origin of his mother and her flight from National Socialism was mentioned in the announcement of his appointment.

Inside the General Box and Paper
company works in Treforest
(© JHASW/George Schoenmann)

FROM 'IDLE FARCE' TO 'GREAT FUN': PAUL AND GEORGE SCHOENMANN AND ENTREPRENEURSHIP IN SOUTH WALES

The story of the Schoenmann family is one of hard work, innovation and entrepreneurship. Paul Schoenmann was able to re-establish his company in one of the Special Areas in South Wales after being forced out of Austria in 1938–39. He established a successful factory, employed many Welsh workers and his family became part of the fabric of local life, which included a large circle of refugee industrialists. Like all businesses there were ups and downs but their existence helped transform the local social and economic landscape. Paul's son George Schoenmann continued the business career of his father, establishing Electrical Spare Parts before his retirement. He still lived near Cardiff in 2022.

There is intense debate on the main motivation for the British government's refugee and immigration policies of the 1930s and 1940s. Some feel it was motivated by the desire to save as many people as possible from persecution, others argue that it was not humanitarian concern that motivated the British government but calculated self-interest. In the case of adult refugees, priority was given to those who could either plug a gap in the supply of labour, for example in the case of employment in domestic service, or create new employment opportunities, in the case of attracting entrepreneurs willing to set up businesses in deprived areas. In 1934, the British government had passed the Special Areas (Development and Improvement) Act with the aim to increase the employment prospects in areas of deprivation and high unemployment and had identified Lanarkshire, North East England, West Cumberland and South Wales as the four Special Areas that were in need of assistance because of their high unemployment rate and deep-seated poverty. This was especially true for those residents who were not able to work in the traditional industries of the areas, which in the case of South Wales was, of course, coal mining and steel production. The initiative received 2 million pounds of funding, an amount that was immediately criticised for being insufficient. Many claimed that the amount was only enough for the government to be able to say that they cared about these areas rather than achieve wider and lasting change. There were also doubts about the initiative's effectiveness. Aneurin Bevan, the Welsh Labour Party politician, called the Act an 'idle and empty farce'.

Of course, the problems caused by deprivation and unemployment were well known locally and the local authorities in South Wales and Monmouthshire had already established an Industrial Development Council. The new Special Areas Act provided this Council with new impetus for their efforts, but it soon became clear that they faced an uphill struggle to attract British industrialists to the area as the funding was not supposed to be used as a direct subsidy for any for-profit business. Despite strong efforts advertising the initiative, it looked like it would fail completely. However, the Special Areas Act was amended in 1936 and 1937, and direct subsidies to businesses were offered and the government funded the establishment of industrial estates such as the Treforest Estate near Pontypridd, which provided modern facilities and infrastructure like transport links to the budding entrepreneurs. Economic historians think of the Special Areas Act as not very effective. It did, however, provide opportunities for refugee industrialists. Most of them tried to establish a new enterprise in the UK while they were still living in Central Europe. From the British governmental point of view, refugees were ideally suited to this policy: they were experienced entrepreneurs with good connections to Central Europe and further afield. Factories set up by refugee industrialists on the Treforest Estate included Aero Zip, Pearl Paint and Lion Leather. Welsh officials from the industrial estate and the Development Council worked tirelessly to help them, and the companies received start-up funds, rate and tax rebates, and other help. It is interesting that there were no obstacles to providing subsidies to refugee businesses, as in other areas of professional or everyday life the government was very much against paying any financial assistance to refugees. These financial aids enabled the diversification of industries in the local areas and so, to some extent at least, the Special Area initiative could be considered a success.

Paul Schoenmann was one of the entrepreneurs who took the opportunity to create a pathway to leave National Socialist persecution behind by establishing a business on the Treforest Industrial Estate. Paul was born in 1899 into a Jewish family in Vienna. He served as an Artillery Officer in the Austrian Army during the First World War and he ran the family's cigarette paper business together with his father. Paul was responsible for the sales side of the business. His wife Emmie's Jewish family was originally from Galicia (a region that is now split between Poland and Ukraine) but they had established themselves in Vienna like many other Eastern European Jewish migrants seeking economic betterment. Paul and Emmie Schoenmann fled with their young son and daughter from Vienna to Cardiff in 1939. Businessman Paul had set up The General Paper and Box Manufacturing Company on the Treforest Estate in 1938 before his eventual emigration – it had become clear after the Anschluss that the persecution of Jewish citizens in Austria was increasing.

Soon after the annexation of Austria, in March 1938, many Jewish-owned businesses were Aryanised, meaning that Jewish owners and managers were replaced by non-Jewish men and women, often without any, or minimal, compensation. This seems to have happened to the Schoenmann cigarette paper business. In most cases, Jewish owners were removed from the Aryanised business immediately, but Paul Schoenmann was actually initially prevented from emigrating, as the competitor who had taken over the business wanted to rely on his expertise a little longer and persuaded the authorities to deny Paul permission to emigrate. Eventually, in April 1939, the new owner of the business informed the authorities that Paul's services were no longer required and the family managed to leave Vienna. Their escape had little in common with the desperate scramble to get away that we know about from some refugees. The family went by taxi to Vienna airport and took a KLM flight to Britain. However, initially all they had in available cash was £5 and they had to live in rented accommodation in the Whitchurch area of Cardiff. A few months later, the family found out that they had been lucky and their private possessions, their furniture and other belongings arrived in Cardiff safely. The shipment had been arranged by a friend of the family.

Paul's father and mother did not wish to leave Vienna. This was not untypical for older middle-class Jews. Some could not face the idea of a new start in a foreign country, some did not want to be a hindrance to their children's new lives, others thought that the Nazis would not harm old people, and some believed that things would not get as bad as was rumoured. Unfortunately, they were wrong. It is very difficult to understand these decisions with hindsight, but the cruelty and scale of the Holocaust is still very difficult to comprehend over 80 years after the end of the Second World War and with all our historical knowledge. It is therefore not surprising that it was difficult to anticipate for people in 1939. Paul's father died in Vienna in 1941 of a heart attack. His mother was deported and murdered in one of the notorious gas lorries in Chelmno extermination camp. The family had managed to receive news of the grandparents via a relative in New York as the US entered the war and thus knew of their grandfather's death. These messages eventually ceased and the Schoenmann family did not find out about the grandmother's fate until after 1945. However, she had continued to correspond with her youngest sister in Shanghai and these more detailed letters were found in a loft long after the war and eventually published as a book by a relative.

Paul Schoenmann had already registered his interest in establishing a business on the Treforest Estate before his departure from Vienna. He established the company in 1938 because he planned to emigrate after the annexation of Austria in early 1938 but, as discussed, he was initially prevented from leaving. Because he was not able to bring any assets and savings with him, he could not establish a business on his own. The Treforest Estate and Industrial Council authorities connected him with Hermann Toffler, a refugee from Czechoslovakia who had been able to bring some of his money with him and wanted to invest in a business. They connected them further to Rudolf Wilheim, whose expertise was in the production of cardboard boxes and who was looking for a partner. Schoenmann and Wilheim successfully applied for their company to receive start-up funds and for a factory to be established on the Treforest Estate. The necessary machinery was bought in France in 1938 and shipped to Cardiff. By the time the Schoenmanns came to Cardiff in 1939, the factory was already set up and ready to go. The factory was almost a complete replica of the one the Schoenmann family had had in Vienna, certainly on the cigarette paper side of the business. The paper started off as large rolls of paper. It was cut up into bobbins, and then it was folded and cut and placed in cigarette paper booklets. As Paul had been managing the sales side of the business in Vienna, he was able to solicit orders immediately. The Cardiff company sold cigarette paper to distributors in Portugal, South Africa and in many other countries. Their main customer, however, was the Rizla company in London. In some ways, Rizla was a competitor but was not able to meet the current demand, so they bought from General Paper and Box. Business boomed during the Second World War as many people rolled their own cigarettes to save money. As well as producing cigarette papers, the company also produced cardboard boxes, such as high-quality shoeboxes and gift boxes. However, this side of the business did not do so well during the war, as not as many goods were produced that required to be sold in high-quality boxes.

Many items were mended or sold second-hand. In 1943, Paul Schoenmann and Rudolf Wilheim parted company after a disagreement and Wilheim relocated the box manufacturing part of the operation to Ynysybwl.

After the start of the Second World War, the UK government's policy of interning foreign nationals (which was stepped up in May 1940) had a negative impact on many refugee-led enterprises. However, neither the classification process – into different categories according to the likely danger individuals might pose to the UK – nor its implementation were consistent throughout the different areas in the UK. Paul Schoenmann avoided internment; the fact that he was indispensable to a business employing dozens of British, or rather Welsh workers, was considered a sufficient reason in his case. Another threat to the viability or even the survival of a refugee business was the fact that the government could requisition a part of a factory, or even a whole one, if it deemed this necessary for the war effort. This could lead to businesses having to cease trading but in the case of General Paper and Box there were no ill effects. During the war years the company had a toolroom that made parts for the Ministry of Defence – mostly for Rolls Royce Spitfire engines. In this way, the company made a direct contribution to the British war effort.

Despite the obvious financial advantages the Schoenmann family had, compared to many other families who were not able to establish themselves in their chosen profession or even find jobs at all, their integration into life in Wales was not smooth in all aspects of everyday life. George Schoenmann was five years old when he arrived in Wales. He remembers being allowed to play in some areas of the factory when he accompanied his father on a Saturday or during school holidays. The family initially lived in rented rooms in Whitchurch, then a separate village, now a suburb of Cardiff. When their financial situation improved, they were able to move to a family house in Whitchurch, an area that was not too expensive but felt quite middle class. Whitchurch's then status as a separate village, and not a part of the capital city, proved an advantage when Cardiff became a restricted area that refused entry to some refugees.

Initially George Schoenmann went to a state primary school. He remembers this being very difficult as he could not speak English; he was excluded by the other pupils for being foreign and called names:

'... I went to the state school, and that didn't work out very well 'cos ... I couldn't speak English and I was teased mercilessly ... I call it bullying, it wasn't physical, it was just they would call me names, Jerry was the favourite one 'cos of course the war had just started and they would run around pretending to be airplanes as little children did in those days with arms outstretched, [laughs], making noises and I was always the ... Messerschmitt which got shot at. Anyway ... it wasn't very pleasant and the fact that I couldn't speak a word of English, of course, and no effort was really made to include me in the lessons, so every day at break time, at ten o'clock I sneaked out through the gate and ran home.'

As a consequence, George started to abscond from school during the morning break. After this had gone on for three or four months – the school did not notice or did not care – he was caught by his aunt, another refugee living in the UK who had come to visit his mother unexpectedly. The aunt found George sitting on the railway bank watching the trains during the morning of a school day and, of course, told his mother. George's parents were clearly shocked about what had happened – and also about the fact that it had taken them so long to find out about it – and quickly moved their son to a small private school called Masefield House. This school was closed down after about a year and George was moved to another small private school, Lamorna, which he attended until he was eleven. He passed the eleven-plus exam but was not allocated the grammar school he wanted to go to and his parents decided to send him to Christ College in Brecon, a public school. George boarded there for seven years and thereafter only came home in school holidays.

The family initially spoke German with each other all the time, although obviously after a few months most family members spoke English as well and used it outside the home. The only one who did not learn English was Schoenmann's mother-in-law who had arrived in Wales from Vienna three months after the rest of the family in July 1939. It seems likely that Paul and Emmie had managed to secure her a visa for the UK by guaranteeing her upkeep and arguing that she would join their household. As an older woman who did not go out to work and only mixed with other German-speaking refugees, she did not learn much English. Paul and his mother-in-law did not get on well and, in 1950, Emmie's mother emigrated to Brazil where Emmie's brother lived. As there was no one in the home who did not speak English, English became more and more the dominant language in the Schoenmann household.

Paul returned to Vienna immediately after the end of the Second World War. He went back in 1946 after obtaining his British citizenship and being issued with a British passport. Like Berlin, Vienna was divided into four sectors, allocated to the Soviet, American, British and French Occupation powers. As luck would have it, the family's former cigarette paper factory was in the British zone, and Paul was therefore told that he could take possession of the family's factory again. In most cases, this process was a lot more complicated, and could take decades. After all that had happened, Paul clearly had no desire to return his family to Vienna and run the factory in person, so he contracted the people who had taken over the factory to stay on as tenants and pay him rent. This they did and the Schoenmann family received a regular income from the factory. The only complication for the Schoenmanns was that the rent was paid in Austrian schillings, which they could not take out of Austria or exchange for another currency. The family seems to have used this money to spend many holidays in Austria over the next ten years. After this, the Austrian company managers wanted to buy the factory buildings and the family agreed to sell to them. There were other business interests that members of the Schoenmann family managed to retrieve, such as a share in a cinema in Vienna. This was later converted into a supermarket and rented to a well-known Austrian supermarket chain.

Back in Wales, after the war a new factory building for cigarette paper manufacturing was built behind the original factory on the Treforest Estate and business was buoyant. However, the strength of the cigarette paper business led to Rizla seeing the company as a dangerous competitor rather than a collaborator. Rizla made a takeover bid and the other directors who were investors and not actively involved in managing the business accepted this bid. Paul Schoenmann, who was the managing director and the only one actively involved in running the business, did not want to sell. He was outvoted and had to accept the takeover bid. Paul was given a five-year contract by Rizla to continue to manage the business and worked for them as a manager until 1951. Rizla paid him out his shares and gave him the rest of his salary as a lump sum and even gave him his car. Paul was financially secure, but it was difficult for him to accept retirement at the early age of 52.

In an interview in 2018, Paul's son George stated that his father and other fellow refugee industrialists were not especially keen to establish their businesses and their new lives in Wales and that most of them would rather have lived and worked in London or near one of the larger urban centres. However, as they needed the support offered via the Special Areas Act, South Wales was considered a preferable option to the north-east of England or Scotland. Looking back from a 21st century point of view, it does not look like this reluctance persisted for too long. While a lot of businesses needed initial help and also help with hiring and training workers, most refugee companies became financially viable and even successful. The refugee industrialists and their families integrated into Welsh life: not untypically, the older generation's social life was more focused on their own community. Paul and Emmie Schoenmann had a recurring weekly social calendar and met at different refugee families' houses; for example, they met every Friday at the Toefflers, his business partner. But the next generation socialised much more widely.

It is clear the innovation of the refugee industrialists contributed to a diversification of industries in the area and provided employment opportunities, especially to women, younger workers and workers with disabilities. A study in 1941 found that by May 1940 there were 55 refugee factories on the Treforest Estate employing 1,800 workers. And as we will see below many of these businesses lasted until the 1980s and further new enterprises were established by the children of the initial refugee industrialists.

Paul Schoenmann's son George left Christ College in Brecon, having gained the qualifications to go to university; he wanted to study engineering, which he was very passionate about. Unfortunately, because his marks in mathematics were not considered good enough, he was asked to sit further maths exams before being accepted on an honours programme in engineering at Cardiff University. George managed to pass these exams and was admitted to the first year on a BSc in Engineering but passing maths exams remained a problem for him. In the end, he met his future wife Jill at a Saturday dance, his priorities changed and he did not complete his university degree.

Having become a naturalised British citizen, George was then called up to do National Service and for his basic training he was sent to RAF Bridgnorth in Shropshire. George did not find basic training too difficult because of his public school education. There, he had been in the Cadet Force and his days had always been quite regimented. He originally wanted to join the photography unit –

photography was his hobby – but he did not pass the entry test. He then trained as a radio fitter, which suited him well because of the subjects he had studied at university and school. He spent five months at RAF Compton Bassett in Wiltshire, and then he was posted to Northern Ireland and East Anglia, a long way from Jill who was at Art College in Gloucester. National Service matured George and he saw parts of the UK he might not have seen otherwise in the late 1950s. He and Jill were married in a church in Llandough.

This is an interesting development: George's school had allowed refugee Jews to refrain from joining Christian services or Christian religious instruction; nevertheless, the public school system clearly had an effect on George. Despite identifying as Jewish to this day, it was not important to him to be part of a Jewish community. George felt that the Welsh Jewish community in Cardiff had not been as helpful to the new refugees in the 1930s and 1940s than they might have been, which put him off.

After Paul stopped working for Rizla, he was part of a number of unsuccessful ventures but eventually founded a furniture factory in Bridgend, again in partnership with Mr Toeffler who had been a fellow director at Rizla. Paul received his pay out from Rizla as did Toeffler, and they went into equal partnership in a company called ESTO Products, which specialised in the manufacturing of kitchen cabinets. In 1958, when George finished his National Service, his father and his partner were able to take him on as a sales representative. George travelled all over the country selling kitchen furniture, but the pay was not good and he had to pay for his own travel and overnight accommodation. Thus, he took on another sales job selling fireside chairs to furniture shops at the same time. When George's father became ill and was unable to work for six months, ESTO went into bankruptcy. George then went to work for Tom Adler whom he had been at school with and who was the son of another refugee industrialist at a company named, interestingly, Welsh Products Limited. From the early 1960s onwards, George worked for a number of companies who were still owned by refugee families or had been founded by them, including Western Gloves, Burlington Gloves, and Stewart's Fabric Factory. He changed jobs when he was approached by another company's managers or owners, or just fancied a change and 'got a copy of the *Echo* and there was another job'. George and Jill had two daughters and moved from Merthyr to Llandough to Cardiff during those years.

Eventually George founded his own company, Electrical Spare Parts, in 1979. Initially, he ran it from the coalhouse at the back of their home; however, it went from strength to strength to become an international business. George was clearly a talented business and salesman like his father and his business survived several recessions. The company had 30 employees at its peak and only closed after George retired in 2003 aged 70. Even then, George did not really retire as he continued to run a battery company called Espex Batteries until he was nearly 80. In this way, father and son were part of the fabric of the community of owners of small to medium businesses in South Wales for over sixty years. One of George's daughters still owns a shop in Penarth and George was still helping out in 2018.

Paul Schoenmann might only have chosen the Special Area of South Wales and the Treforest Estate for his cigarette paper business because of the financial incentives available but his son George enjoyed his working life in Wales: he felt that running Electrical Spare Parts and competing on the international market from their base in Cardiff 'was great fun.' In this instance, the Schoenmann family's combination of altruistic and self-interested reasons for rescuing innovative and experienced refugee business people and their families from National Socialist persecution worked out for the refugee families and for Wales and the Welsh people. It has taken a long time for the refugee entrepreneurs' contribution to be properly acknowledged and research in this area is only just starting to gather momentum. The refugee businesses on the Treforest Estate employed 1,800 people at their peak during the Second World War and immediately afterwards. This clearly had a significant and positive effect on the economic landscape of South Wales. If the Schoenmann family is anything to go by, refugees continue to have a lasting impact as subsequent generations also set up enterprises, some of which are still active.

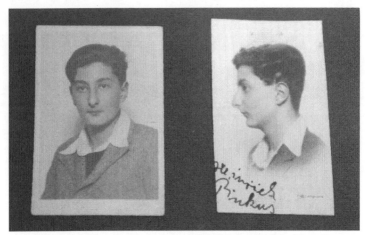

Heinrich Pinkus, latterly known as Heinz Koppel (© Gaby Koppel)

One of Heinz Koppel's paintings (© Gaby Koppel)

INNOVATION IN BUSINESS AND ART:
THE KOPPEL FAMILY

In some cases, wealthy and well-known refugees managed to hang on to some of their privilege even after they had to flee National Socialism. For example, Thomas Mann, the world-famous German author, and winner of the Nobel Prize for Literature in 1929, first emigrated to Switzerland in 1933 and then escaped to the US at the beginning of the Second World War. Mann and his family resettled in California, near Los Angeles in an area called Pacific Palisades which came to signify the comfortable refuge of the wealthy intelligentsia. This stands in stark contrast to the experience of many refugees, some even equally privileged before the Nazi takeover, who had to live in poverty and obscurity.

Most refugees to Wales were neither well known nor wealthy. But some of the refugee industrialists obviously brought with them more money and assets than most. Some had led the international lives of successful businessmen before they suffered persecution. Joachim Koppel was one such entrepreneur who first fled from Germany to Czechoslovakia and then eventually to the UK. With a track record of successful zip-manufacturing all over Europe, he established the company Aero Zip on the Treforest Industrial Estate. Joachim was initially not keen to move to Wales with his family; he felt Wales was too parochial and therefore he kept offices in London and commuted from London to his factory at Treforest. While Cardiff was not able to compete with some of the amenities of European capitals Joachim had frequented before 1939, Alien records show nonetheless that he lived there during the Second World War

Despite Joachim's initial reluctance, his sons and stepsons and their families became part of Welsh society after the end of the Second World War. His son Heinz became an artist and was part of the 56 Group Wales/Grŵp 56 Cymru which was established with the aim to promote modernist art in Wales. His stepson Heinrich worked for Aero Zip as an engineer and brought up his family as part of the émigré community in Cardiff in the 1940s, 1950s, and 1960s. One of Heinrich's daughters, Gaby Koppel, wrote the novel *Reparation* published by Honno and influenced by her memories of growing up in this milieu, and to this day she identifies as Welsh.

Joachim Koppel was born in 1892. He first married Paula and had two sons, Kurt (born 1916) and Heinz (born 1919). In 1930, Joachim and Paula divorced and he married Cilly Koppel, née Cohn. She had also been married before – to Paul Pinkus, with whom she had two children. Cilly's son Heinrich was born in 1922 and his sister Ilse was a year younger. Cilly left Paul Pinkus around 1924 or 1925 when her children were still very small. Cilly and Joachim seem to have had a passionate relationship even before they were married. Cilly took Joachim's surname, and her son Heinrich subsequently changed his name to Koppel when the family were living in Cardiff.

Joachim Koppel was a businessman with many business interests and a keen interest in technical innovation. In 1913, at 21 years of age, he became a representative for a lead manufacturing business; thereafter, he worked for several other enterprises in the metal business and, by 1920, he was registered as one of the directors of a business in the metal trade in the Tiergarten district of Berlin. Joachim invested a lot of the profits in technical innovations. Some were rather more fruitful than others. For example, a car engine that supposedly ran on crude oil instead of petrol turned out to be a fraud and lost Joachim a fortune. The development of new machines for the manufacturing of zips was a lot more successful. Joachim and a partner patented these machines in many different countries: his partner in Germany, Joachim outside Germany.

Joachim did not sell the patents to the different firms in the different countries but became a partner in those companies that wanted to make these machines. In this way, Joachim acquired business interests in Poland, Romania, Austria, Belgium, France, Italy, Czechoslovakia, and the UK. Through these business activities, Joachim became a very wealthy man and the international connections he forged would be very advantageous come the rise of the Third Reich. Joachim's business success meant that the Koppel family were able to move into increasingly more lavish apartments in Berlin every few years and that they were gradually able to acquire a cook, a nanny, and eventually a chauffeur to drive the family's Mercedes.

Joachim was warned that he was in danger after Adolf Hitler's rise to power in 1933. He was a prominent Jewish businessman, and certainly attracted attention from people who were envious of his success. It is therefore not surprising that the National Socialists wanted to harm him, and possibly get their hands on some of his wealth. By March 1933, Joachim had emigrated to Prague. His stepson Heinrich later remembered that arguments broke out amongst the members of both sides of his extended biological and stepfamily. Some felt that the family should leave Germany immediately, some felt that they should stay put as the adverse political climate would soon blow over. Always decisive, Joachim opted to leave immediately.

Joachim had stakes in two factories in German-speaking areas of Czechoslovakia, one near Chabařovice and one in Teplice-Šanov. He clearly hoped that he could continue with his business interests from his new base. Initially this was successful, and he continued to travel all over Europe, with the obvious exception of Germany. Around two years after Joachim's move, the rest of the family – including his sons and his ex-wife Paula – also relocated. Paula was chronically ill, suffering from severe arthritis and was by the late 1930s bedridden. She fled from Berlin to Czechoslovakia two years after Joachim, but when the family moved on to the UK, she did not travel with them. She might have felt that another move would be too difficult bearing in mind her state of health. She might have hoped that the Nazis would not harm her. It is also possible that the UK authorities were unwilling to admit this very ill woman despite Joachim and the family being able to guarantee financial support for her. Tragically, Paula was later deported to Theresienstadt and murdered in Treblinka.

Obviously, all the older Koppel family members knew this but it seems that the younger generation did not. Gaby Koppel, the daughter of Heinrich Koppel, who was born in 1957 in Cardiff and works as a journalist and TV producer, was surprised that she only found out about the fate of her uncles' mother in her forties. In an interview, she said she was surprised she had never asked her older relatives what happened to Paula.

Czechoslovakia provided a refuge for the Koppels, and a base for Joachim to further develop his business, but family members' lives were clearly overshadowed by the darkening clouds of political change in Europe. While the elder son Kurt managed to pass his school leaving exams at his Czech grammar school, Heinz was not a successful student. His father tried to convince him to attend school and when this did not work, he tried to engage home tutors, but according to his brother, Heinz simply refused to go to school or pay attention. All Heinz was interested in was developing his painting. In 1936, Kurt and Heinz moved to London as life in Central Europe was getting increasingly difficult. Kurt worked in the UK firm that was part of his father's zip manufacturing emporium. The UK business had been run by Joachim's brother, Leon Koppel, who had already emigrated to the UK in 1932. Heinz Koppel studied painting at the Contemporary School for Painting and Drawing in London, which was led by the expressionist painter Martin Bloch, a German-Jewish refugee artist who had also fled to the UK. A year later, in 1937, Joachim asked his sons to return to Prague for a few months. This journey did not turn out to be entirely straightforward. Heinz's passport had been withdrawn by the German Embassy in London when he had presented it for renewal on 1 March 1937. The German Embassy argued that Heinz was no longer a German citizen because his parents were no longer German citizens. Fortunately, the British authorities furnished the now stateless Heinz with a temporary travel document.

All the family members were now united in Prague again but travelling was clearly becoming increasingly difficult. Joachim therefore bought new passports and the necessary naturalisation documentation for himself, Cilly and all four of their children from the Costa Rican Embassy in Prague. At the same time other Koppel relatives managed to flee to Italy. Joachim, Cilly and the children joined them there. They seem to have spent a number of months in Mergozzo in Italy. Family photographs from the time look like holiday snaps. But the mood must have been tense. Clearly Joachim could not quite decide on his next move. Where should he relocate to and where should the Koppel businesses be directed from? Joachim fancied Antwerp and this is where he travelled to with his wife, Heinz and his younger stepchildren. His eldest son, Kurt, travelled to London via Brussels, and eventually managed to convince his father to establish his base there and not in Antwerp. The funding that the Special Areas programme (discussed in the earlier chapter on Paul and George Schoenmann) was providing made a difference in this decision-making process. Consequently, Joachim established the company Aero Zip Fasteners Ltd and its factory on the Treforest Estate, where it would eventually become hugely successful; by 1965, the company contributed one third of all British zip exports.

Despite his business success, before and after his flight, Joachim's life was not trouble free. He had problems with his digestive system and a lot of correspondence between him and Cilly concerns the details of this ailment and what foods he was trying to avoid. Unusually, both Heinrich and his sister Ilse were interned on the Isle of Man, he was seventeen and she was sixteen. Researchers believe they were two of the youngest individual internees. Some women internees lived with their children in the Isle of Man camp, but enemy aliens under 18 were not normally interned.

Joachim's stepson Heinrich was not only interned, but he was also among the young men who were sent to Canada. For Heinrich, this experience was less traumatic then one might expect. Heinrich almost saw his time on the Isle of Man as a form of informal university. He recalled that he learned a lot about different subjects such as music – he heard the Amadeus Quartet play – he learned to play bridge, which became his lifelong passion, and he learned other elements about Central European culture from the older internees, some of whom were well-known academics and writers, artists, and musicians. He felt comfortable in this milieu and the older internees looked after him. Heinrich was a man with a positive attitude even when things were challenging. He felt that the British were justified in interning foreigners and understood the fear that some might be German spies or foreign agitators. He had a more difficult time in Canada, where he experienced extreme cold and struggled with the meagre rations.

Fortunately, he came to no harm, and after 18 months he returned to the UK. He attended the Institute of Mechanical Engineers which was part of the University of London. He studied mechanical and electrical engineering and he finished at the top of his class. Heinrich had the interest in technology and engineering that both his father and stepfather lacked. Despite his experience running manufacturing companies and investing in technological innovations, Joachim was not technically minded himself. Heinrich used to joke that it was pointless when his stepfather looked under the bonnet of his car if it had broken down, as he would hardly recognise an engine. However, Joachim was aware that the business needed engineering experts, and both his eldest son Kurt and his stepson stepped up to the task. Heinz's talent clearly lay in a completely different area, namely fine arts. (As we will see, Harry Weinberger, a cousin of the Koppels, also disliked engineering and preferred to pursue a career as an artist.) In addition to his studies,

Heinrich trained as a toolmaker at Aero Zip on the Treforest Estate. Eventually, he ended up as the chief engineer of the company and other family members also worked there.

Aero Zip brought significant innovation to Wales as well as employing local people. This had been the aim of the Special Areas scheme. The areas clearly needed investment, and local people needed jobs. Pontypridd had had an unemployment rate of 53 per cent in 1936. By April 1939, 78 companies had established factories on the Treforest estate, of these 49 were refugee-owned. During the war, Aero Zip made zips for uniforms and equipment for the armed forces as well. All the family contributed to the war effort. One family member even became a member of the Home Guard; in fact, it became a family joke as his relatives tried to imagine this fat, older man in a British Army uniform riding on a bicycle in the Treforest area, speaking with a German accent and aiming to defend his adopted home country.

But refugee families, such as the Koppel family and the Schoenmann family – also discussed in this book – did not just change the manufacturing industry of Wales forever. They also brought some Central European customs to Wales and formed a small enclave in Cardiff. Heinrich Koppel married Edith, a Jewish refugee from Budapest, who had survived in hiding and then come to the UK after the Second World War. Their daughter Gaby Koppel remembers growing up with many other children of refugees in the neighbourhood. She recalls them having coffee and cake together, holding parties and playing cards. Gaby's parents still had a sense of Cardiff being a bit of a backwater as they had previously lived in major European capital cities: Berlin and Prague in Heinrich's case, and Budapest and Paris in Edith's. Edith liked telling stories such as her visiting a specialist wine shop in South Wales and asking for a rosé and the shop assistant not knowing what a rosé was. In some ways, this meant that Heinrich and Edith remained focused on the Continent, still admiring German culture. This was not unusual amongst refugees at the time, despite feeling that the UK was their permanent home now. It is possible that the experience of not being accepted in Germany, of being discriminated against, and of being persecuted, made the culture look more desirable, something one wanted to be part of but was refused entry to. However, this veneration of the great European capitals and their way of life was also in keeping with hierarchical 20th century ideas of high culture. For Heinrich and Edith, Welsh culture remained marginal and somewhat parochial; it could not compete with that of their native countries. Heinrich ended up as a cultural mediator and translator. He left Aero Zip and, after running his own business, became a consultant and translator, helping technical installation crews overcome communication difficulties with the companies they were working for and translating any technical documents that were needed. Gaby's father preferred to buy his suits in Germany and her mother loved shopping at German supermarkets such as Aldi and Lidl (before you could do so in Wales) because the products were good value and the soups and spices made by Maggi and Knorr suited her Central European palate. Gaby remembered that once her parents' luggage was searched when coming back to the UK after a post-war trip to Germany, and that the officials were incredulous that somebody should wish to bring in instant soups and sauces, and suspicious that the packets of powdery substance might be something else altogether.

The downside to their parents' foreignness was also experienced by Gaby as a child. She felt ill at ease bringing friends to her home in Rhiwbina in Cardiff after school as her mother seemed very loud compared to her friends' mothers, and the food they had for their evening meal was so different from the food her friends had. Like many children of immigrants, Gaby kept her home life separate from her outside life. Every Sunday the former refugees would have a get together in someone's house. The parents would get the children to Cheder – religious instruction sessions for Jewish children – and then all meet up for coffee. Most men would be refugee industrialists or working for one of the companies that had been set up by refugee industrialists. The men all sat in the front room, and the family who hosted the gathering got out their best china and made some very strong black coffee; the men would discuss, business, politics, and their hobbies. There was a strong ethos of community and of giving each other business and buying from shops or businesses run by other former refugees – of mutual support.

One place where Gaby could bring both sides of her life closer was at the Jewish Youth Club, Ner Tamid, based at the Reform Synagogue in Moira Terrace in Cardiff. There, young people from Anglo-Jewish, Welsh-Jewish and Continental Jewish backgrounds met. Initially, the leaders of this club were Michael Moritz and his sister Clare. The Moritzes' parents were also refugees from National Socialism. When Michael stepped down to concentrate on his university application, Gaby remembers being worried that they would not find anyone as good to replace him as Youth Club leader. Today Sir Michael Moritz is a Welsh billionaire venture capitalist and philanthropist. Gaby clearly saw his leadership potential even in those early days.

Gaby herself left Wales to study at the University of Sussex but was keen to return when she started to apply for jobs as a journalist. She applied for jobs on the *Western Mail*, with the BBC in Cardiff and on the *South Wales Argus* in Newport. Today she lives in North London, and works as a writer, journalist and television producer. She defines herself as Welsh, British and from a family with a refugee background.

As already discussed, Heinrich's stepbrother Heinz Koppel was not at all interested in gaining academic qualifications nor in being involved in the family business. His main interest was art and he became a painter and art teacher. After studying with Bloch in London, and meeting the Welsh artist Cedric Morris, he moved to Dowlais, near Merthyr Tydfil, in 1944 to teach at the Dowlais Settlement School. The school had been founded by the sculptor

John Dennithorne and changed many local people's lives from 1928 onwards. It provided classes for unemployed workers in wide-ranging subjects from English literature to carpentry and also tried to help with practical problems such as housing.

By the 1940s, the local organisers of the school had decided to form a group for local artists and supporters, which became the Merthyr Arts Society. Its aim was to establish an artists' studio and employ a full-time artist-in-residence who would spearhead a local artistic movement. Many local people remember Heinz to this day and it was certainly part of a rejuvenation of a distinct Welsh art movement including 56 Group Wales/Grŵp 56 Cymru (discussed later).

Heinz was known to several of the artists who had been involved in the settlement school over the years and was brought to Dowlais to be the artist-in-residence and to teach local children and adults. The idea of the classes for adults was to expand people's minds and expand their interest in subjects 'important to the human spirit'. People who were unemployed and suffered from poverty would be able to escape the humdrum of their repetitive and restrictive lives and create their own art. Many local people in the area remember either watching Heinz paint in his studio or attended his classes. His widow, Pip, described Heinz as an eccentric but approachable person who was interested in his pupils: 'He was interested to see what people who came to paint chose to paint. He painted them and they painted what they found.'

Heinz had married fellow refugee artist Renate Fischl in 1949. Fischl, also known as Pip Koppel, was born in Dresden and had studied at the East Anglian School of Painting and Drawing. Cedric Morris had recommended that she visit Heinz in Dowlais and they met in December 1948. Two months later they were married. The couple had five children: Hanno (born in 1950), Ruth (1952), Siân Melanie (1955), Gideon (1960) and Jessica Edith (1963).

Heinz painted magnificent portraits of his children, but the surrounding countryside of South Wales was also an important subject of his art, even before he moved to Dowlais. The sketches he made with his cousin Harry Weinberger (discussed in a later section on Harry) served as an inspiration for many of his works. After moving to Dowlais, he also started to paint the decaying industrial areas. He was interested in psychoanalysis and his paintings show mystical influences, often bordering on the fantastic. His murdered mother and the Nazi past is a motif in a series of paintings.

His paintings, influenced by the German Expressionist movement, were being noticed in British and refugee artists' circles. His work was included at Jack Bilbo's prestigious Modern Art Gallery of London in exhibitions of the 1950s and 1960s that included work by artists such as Jankel Adler, Oskar Kokoschka and Kurt Schwitters.

Heinz stayed in Dowlais for twelve years. In 1956, he was one of the founding members of the 56 Group Wales/Grŵp 56 Cymru, which was formed by artists living and working in Wales to promote modern art and show the world that Welsh art was not, as often assumed, conservative and lacking in modern influences. The group felt that the selection of works for exhibition was often dominated by members of selection committees who were not based in Wales and that most art critics never ventured beyond London. Prior to 1956, Wales had no private galleries. The group was also keen to promote Welsh art internationally. Heinz's paintings were included at the 56 Group-dominated show in Washington DC in 1965 and the 56 Group Wales show in Dublin in 1968. Unsurprisingly, their efforts were not appreciated by all. Welsh artist Kyffin Williams called members of the group 'English carpetbaggers' who did not make it in London and therefore came to Wales to the detriment of Welsh-born artists like himself. It is not known whether Koppel's heritage as a German Jewish refugee attracted specific criticism or exempted him from this criticism.

Somewhat ironically, 1956 was also the year in which Heinz and his family left Dowlais and moved to London and Liverpool where he continued to work as an art teacher. It was during this time that his work began to be regularly exhibited in London galleries. However, Wales clearly remained very important to Heinz. In 1969, the family bought a farm in Cwmerfyn, near Aberystwyth, and moved there permanently in 1974. Heinz had become disillusioned with teaching, believing that art teaching might be a futile endeavour. Instead of teaching, he now worked on his farm while remaining active as an artist. His later work included experimentation with various materials such as fibreglass and resin. Heinz died suddenly, aged only 61, on 1 December 1980. Some of Heinz's and Pip's children and grandchildren have become Welsh speakers and still live in Ceredigion. His son, Gideon Koppel, is a film maker and the director of *Sleep Furiously*, a documentary set in Cwmerfyn and focusing on the landscape and population changes of this small farming community in mid Wales. The film was influenced by Gideon's conversations with the Austrian writer and film director Peter Handke and tells a story of endings and new beginnings which can be connected to his family's history as well as life in Wales. After the rise in National Socialism, the family's established life was forcibly curtailed in Germany and Czechoslovakia and they had to move countries repeatedly. After 1945, Heinz moved between Wales and England several times, these moves sparking new impetus for his artistic endeavours.

The first exhibition of Heinz's works in Germany was held nearly 30 years after his death at Berlin's Centrum Judaicum, running from August 2009 to January 2010. German critics compared his early work with Max Liebermann and his late work with Francis Bacon and spoke about the fragmentary strangeness of his work. Inevitably, the newspaper reviews of the exhibition focused on his biography and the fate of his murdered mother, Paula. One critic felt that the strong contours of his paintings were a way to root the painter's existence in a foreign land. Another felt that his paintings showed that Heinz was never really at home in Wales. I think this critic was mistaken. While the members of the first generation might not have chosen to live in Wales, Heinz clearly chose to live in Ceredigion and make it his home. Members of the current generation still live and work in Ceredigion. Writer and journalist Gaby Koppel lives in London but defines herself first and foremost as Welsh. The Koppel family's story is a Welsh story.

Anton Hundsdorfer on top of Wilde Kaiser
mountain (© Ernie Hunter)

Fanny and Bertl Höchstetter after dismissal from
civil service, 1933 (© Ernie Hunter)

LOVE AND POLITICS IN LLANGOLLEN: FANNY HÖCHSTETTER AND ANTON HUNDSDORFER

This is the story of Fanny Höchstetter, who was Jewish and entered the UK on a domestic service permit, and Anton Hundsdorfer, who was persecuted as a communist by the National Socialist regime and had to flee several times under dramatic circumstances. They met, fell in love, and married in Llangollen. Their story highlights the difficulties for women refugees on domestic service permits and the solidarity among women in Wales. It also shows the influence of politically active refugees on the local political and trade union landscape of the Welsh timber industry.

Fanny Höchstetter was born into a Jewish family in 1902, in the small market town of Laupheim in Southern Germany. The local Jewish and Catholic communities had been well-integrated for a long time and Jewish citizens were leading members of local institutions, associations, and clubs. Because of this, Fanny found it difficult to believe that the Nazi government would last and be able to control all areas of life. She believed that the normal democratic order would be restored, and therefore didn't leave Germany until it was almost too late. Her son Ernie Hunter describes his mother as determined to stay initially while her sister wanted to get out of Germany:

'Tante Bertl – wanted to leave very early after Hitler came to power. But my mother was determined to see Hitler out. Höchstetters – that's the family name – [...] had been German for hundreds of years, and I do mean hundreds of years.'

Fanny had attended the local Jewish school, while her sister Bertl attended the local Catholic school – all schools were selective above a certain age and thus the apparently random choice of schools may have been down to this, but it also shows that their parents did not mind too much about the religious orientation when it came to academic education. Both were talented students and they had successful careers. Fanny became a senior civil servant for the Postal Service, worked in the city of Stuttgart and enjoyed all the privileges that were attached to a civil service appointment in Germany at the time. This included protection from dismissal (unless convicted of a criminal offence or found guilty of gross misconduct). In April 1933, the Law for the Restoration of a Professional Civil Service was passed. The law did exactly the opposite to what its title suggests: its aim was to oust professional civil servants who were Jewish or of Jewish descent from their positions. Exemptions were only made for Jews who had fought in the First World War. Of course, this was not the case for Fanny, and she was unceremoniously dismissed, aged only 31, on 7 April 1933. This understandably upset her greatly. She was a respected professional woman and expected the normal rules and policies to continue to apply. Due to the new Nazis rules, she had not received a certificate of dismissal as would have been the correct procedure under normal circumstances. She was so insistent she should receive said certificate that she repeatedly requested it from numerous high-ranking civil servants and eventually even travelled to Berlin to see the Minister for Transport and the Postal Service of the Third Reich, Paul Freiherr von Eltz-Rübenach. He initially also refused to issue a certificate but eventually relented and gave her a large handwritten document detailing her dismissal from her position in the postal section of the civil service. This shows Fanny's mindset and determination, and her continued belief that civil and professional life in Germany should be conducted according to the accepted rules. Fanny's sister, Bertl, also worked in the civil service, she too was dismissed and subsequently worked at a Jewish orphanage in nearby Esslingen.

As time passed and the Nazi hold on power became more established, life for Jewish citizens became more difficult and the sisters decided they had to leave Germany. Bertl wrote to a cousin, Carl Laemmle, who had emigrated from Laupheim to the US in 1884 and had become an American citizen in 1889. Laemmle was a very prominent and very wealthy man, a film producer and the co-founder and, until 1934, owner of Universal Pictures in Los Angeles. Bertl asked him for an affidavit which could prove he would support them financially, and they would not cost the American government any money. Laemmle obliged and sent them a very generous $1 million affidavit, which Bertl took to the American consulate in Stuttgart. Despite this guarantee of support, the sisters were low down on the list of people who were to be granted an entry visa for the US. The US had strict immigration controls and numbers were allocated in order of application with few exceptions made.

By 1938, it became clear to the whole family that life in Germany was becoming impossible, and that it could be years before they would be allowed to emigrate to the US. That year, Bertl answered a job advertisement she found in *The Times* newspaper for a maid in an English household. In May 1938, she was the first of the sisters to leave Germany using a visa and work permit given by the UK to those who were able to obtain a position as a domestic servant. Bertl was lucky as she found a good employer who treated her well. She also managed to find a family nearby willing to employ her sister Fanny. In August 1939, Fanny escaped Germany, mere days before the Second World War started. Unfortunately, Fanny was not so lucky with her employer who treated her like a skivvy and did not speak to her unless giving instructions. She was very unhappy.

As the domestic permits were one of the few ways to gain a visa to the UK, many women like Fanny, who would not have considered working in such a job before, agreed to take on employment in domestic service. This inevitably led to frustrations on the side of the employer and the employee. Not being allowed to speak unless spoken to or being forced to eat in the kitchen were alien concepts to Fanny. Added to which, she had no idea how to run an English household, something her employer might not have anticipated. Her uncle had given her a reference praising her domestic skills, but in actual fact she detested cooking and cleaning. The Höchstetter family had had their own housekeepers, who had always been treated well and as part of the family. Her insistence on receiving the appropriate dismissal certificate also demonstrates how important her social status as a professional woman was to Fanny. This certificate was one of the few items she brought with her when she arrived in the UK, other than a letter opener made of pieces of shrapnel from an injury sustained by her father while fighting in the German army in the First World War. Both items are now in possession of their son who uses them for illustrative purposes when giving talks about Holocaust history and his parents' lives.

Despite these difficulties, Fanny was obviously lucky to escape. In 1941, members of the Jewish community who remained in Laupheim, including members of the Höchstetter family, were sent on the first transport from the state of Baden Württemberg for so-called 'Resettlement to the East'. They were deported to Riga in Latvia, where, soon after arrival, most were shot. This was the end of Jewish life in Laupheim to this day. This is the case with many more rural Jewish communities. Many of the more urban ones recovered, especially after migration of Russian Jews to West Germany in the 1980s.

Fanny accepted her new life (despite the fact that it had little in common with her former career as a civil servant), especially after she was allowed to leave her first unpleasant employer. Until the beginning of the Second World War, refugees on domestic permits were not allowed to leave their employers to seek alternative positions, unless a special permission was granted. This left many young women, and especially the more vulnerable ones, at the mercy of cruel employers. They were trapped and had to live and work in bad conditions; in some cases they suffered sexual and violent abuse. After the outbreak of war this rule changed, and Fanny left her employers in the Wirral as quickly as she could to become a chambermaid at the Hand Hotel in Llangollen. Llangollen had around 3,000 inhabitants at the time, and its economic life was dominated by tourism, agriculture and the timber industry. While Fanny found employment in the former, her future husband Anton Hundsdorfer was employed in the latter.

Anton was from a non-practising Catholic family in Eichstätt in Bavaria and, like Fanny, was also born in 1902. He moved with his mother and stepfather to Bohdalice in the Sudetenland area of Czechoslovakia. The Sudetenland was a border area of Czechoslovakia containing a majority ethnic German population. After the Nazis rise to power in 1933, Germany demanded the 'return' of this area and its ethnic German population to the German Reich. Hitler's threats regarding the matter became more virulent as time went by and, at the end of September 1938, the leaders of Britain, France, and Italy gave in and agreed to the German annexation of the Sudetenland – in what is known as the Munich Agreement – in return for assurances from Hitler that Germany would not start a war. On 15 March 1939, Nazi Germany broke the agreement and invaded, and also occupied, the Czech provinces of Bohemia and Moravia.

Anton's life in the 1920s and 1930s had been spent between Germany and the Sudetenland. Anton did not get on with his authoritarian and conservative stepfather and he ran away from home in 1918, aged 16, and relocated to Munich, where, in 1919, he saw the establishment of the short-lived Bavarian Soviet Republic. Its ideals of communism and democracy made a deep impression on Anton. He became a member of the German Communist Party and regularly distributed propaganda material for the party. Anton felt that the Bavarian Soviet Republic was violently destroyed by right-wing forces and he felt these remained a constant threat to the democratic system of the Weimar Republic.

He trained as a joiner and became a master joiner but all his spare time was spent in politics and the dissemination of communist propaganda. He knew prominent members of the German Communist Party and married a fellow communist Klara Holy. In 1927, Klara and Anton had a daughter called Sonia. Tragically, Klara died in 1928 during a second pregnancy. Anton and Sonja lived with Klara's parents and Anton continued to deliver anti-Nazi leaflets throughout Bavaria. He was known to the Bavarian Nazi Party for these activities, and after 1933 he feared for his life. Anton had to go into hiding and left his daughter in the care of her maternal grandparents, not knowing when or if he would see her again. Sonja's uncles, the brothers of her late mother, were also communists, and were imprisoned and tortured in Dachau concentration camp. Anton fled from Bavaria to the Sudetenland. He had always been a keen mountaineer and therefore knew all the lesser known passes that could be used to flee Germany undetected. Initially, he did not stay outside Germany permanently, and continued with his political activities: he returned to Germany periodically via the mountain route smuggling anti-Nazi leaflets from contacts in Czechoslovakia. On the return journey, he smuggled out comrades who needed to flee Germany. This went well for a time but in winter 1933–34, carrying a rucksack full of anti-Nazi leaflets, he ran into a German border patrol. He managed to evade them and got back into Czechoslovakia again but was shot at and hit by a bullet whilst making his escape. After that incident, he did not repeat these dangerous missions and stayed in semi-hiding working on a pig farm. He tried to get a visa to the UK, but initially he was unsuccessful. He had stated on the application that he was a master joiner, and this was not one of the jobs with a labour shortage in the UK. When he pointed out that he had also worked on the pig farm, he was successful as there was a shortage of people willing to carry out more menial agricultural labour at the time.

As in many of the other refugee stories, luck played its part. Anton ended up working for the shipping magnate Michael Bibby on a farm in Worcester. Bibby also owned Hams Hill Farm in the Wirral, which was his pride and joy. As Bibby liked Anton – his training in joinery enabled him to fix things on the farm – he offered him work on his favourite farm and supported him for years to come. When Anton was interned first at Huyton Camp and then on the Isle of Man – which he especially resented as he was housed next to some German Nazis – it was Bibby who managed to get him released. Unfortunately, Anton could not work in Protected Areas and thus could not work in some of Bibby's farms due to their location. He had to stop working for Bibby and agreed to work for the Forestry Commission at Llangollen.

Anton stayed in Llangollen for five years; he met Fanny soon after his arrival and they married three months later. Fanny got pregnant with their first child and gave birth to a son, Peter, in 1942. The women in Llangollen supported her by lending her a pram, baby clothes and other useful items, and also helped her with advice and childcare. Fanny retained very fond memories of the Welsh community and the Welsh landscape. According to their son Ernie, she would talk about how, with its green hills and trees, Llangollen reminded her of her native Southern Germany.

Anton also liked Wales, and it may well have been the community of politically active refugee workers that made him feel at home in Llangollen. The Forestry Commission work in Llangollen was still in the development stages when the refugee workers arrived. The Forestry Commission produced timber structures for the mining industry and other infrastructure projects and was desperate for labour.

Fellow German refugee Gerhard Oertel wrote about the political activities in Llangollen. Oertel describes how he fled to the UK under the care of the Czech Refugee Fund (which might have supported Anton's application as well). Oertel remembers there were about 100 foreign workers, mainly German, Austrian and Czech, working for the Forestry Commission in Llangollen in the summer of 1940. Soon after their arrival, they were threatened with internment. This was met with anger from the refugees as most of them had been active in the anti-Nazi resistance, had been persecuted and had fled because of their anti-Nazi activities; they were most unlikely to turn against their hosts. Some fellow workers and even members of the local police supported them when they protested against this treatment. People in Llangollen had got to know the refugee workers and did not see how they could possibly pose a security risk. Nevertheless, the rules had to be complied with, and most of the foreign workers were interned, either in Huyton internment camp or elsewhere in England. Oertel describes how he protested against this incarceration:

'As soon as I had been committed to the provisional internment camp at Prees Heath near Whitchurch [in North Shropshire], I wrote a letter to Brother William Holmes, General Secretary of the Agricultural Workers' Union, insisting that the German anti-Nazi trade unionists should be released from internment without delay.'

The camp in Prees Heath in Shropshire was guarded by men who were miners from South Wales. Oertel recalled how he was able to befriend them due to common political ideals and that they were willing to smuggle out letters avoiding censorship from the British military authorities. Oertel managed to get released in November 1940 and returned to Llangollen. The Czech Refugee Trust Fund, in the meantime, had rented buildings in Llangollen which served as accommodation for the majority of the workers. The buildings were called the Eifion, the Waverley, and the Craigivar buildings, and some of them had accommodated tourists before the war.

Having been members of trade unions before their flight, the refugee workers soon felt that they needed to organise, and as no trade unions existed in Llangollen, they contacted the secretary of the Agricultural Workers' Union in Shrewsbury and agreed to build up a branch of that union in Llangollen. Initially almost all members were German, Austrian and Czechoslovak refugees. Leonard Wilsham, also a non-local, but a UK citizen, was elected as branch chairman. They tried to recruit more local members, but many workers were from a tenant farming background and they expected to have to go back to this as their only source of income after the end of the war. Therefore, they were scared that becoming a union member would have repercussions for them in the future and were reluctant to join. According to Oertel, it took 18 months before the first local members joined. The emergent Llangollen Branch held monthly meetings. Initially the language of communication was German, since the Czech and Slovak colleagues also spoke it, and even the English chairman understood it. When local men joined, they switched to English. Some small actions in relation to working conditions but also in relation to pay had impressed the local workers. Oertel himself was dissatisfied with the pay and, in 1942, applied to the local Labour Exchange for permission to change his place of employment. This was denied because by then he had worked in the forestry industry for two years and this industry was considered important to the war effort. Oertel did not give up and applied to an industrial tribunal where he was defended by the secretary of the Agricultural Workers' Union of Shrewsbury. His application was rejected for the same reason, but the tribunal ordered that the Forestry Commission should pay him a penny more in wages per hour. As this would have meant that he would receive higher pay than the other sawmill workers at Pentredwr, the Forestry Commission increased the pay of all employees, which naturally impressed the local men.

The foreign workers also integrated into Welsh cultural life. They formed an international choir of forestry workers, which included Welsh, English, Czech, Slovak, Austrian and German singers. They also organised international dances at the town hall in Llangollen which were very popular and attended by up to 250 people. The foreign workers had to apply for special permission if they wanted to be out beyond 11.30 p.m. Apparently, this permission was readily granted on these occasions. The dances must have been a good occasion for people to get to know each other. More than one relationship was formed in Llangollen. Karl Bruckdorfer, a close and lifelong friend of Anton Hundsdorfer, accompanied the choir on his guitar. Like Anton, Bruckdorfer also fell in love, in his case with a Welsh beauty queen, Emily Rastall from Llangollen. Like Fanny and Anton, Karl and Emily also married and stayed in the UK after the war.

After the end of the war, Anton and Fanny decided to leave Wales for greater economic opportunities and moved to the Manchester area. The shipping magnate Bibby helped Anton and Fanny financially to obtain a mortgage and a house. However, it was a bit of a shock to leave Wales behind and settle in the industrial heartlands of England. They had enjoyed the clean air, green hills and trees of Wales; now they had to put up with pollution, urban deprivation and bad housing. Their son Ernie remembers his mother telling of her unhappiness about the new location: Fanny had not been able to see the house before it was bought, and when she arrived with their son Peter, she nearly turned around and went back to Wales. But as before, they made the best of it. Anton worked as a joiner, their second son Ernie was born in 1946, and Fanny supported Anton by using her administrative skills to help set up his joinery business. Ernie remembered that his father had less of a business brain than his mother, and that she was glad when she could set up her own business, a DIY shop, when both sons were a little older.

Immediately after the end of the Second World War, Anton tried to get in touch with his daughter Sonja from his first marriage. He decided to write a letter in German to the Lord Mayor of Munich asking for help to reconnect with his daughter whom he had not heard from since the start of the war. Rather than posting it, which would have been a futile attempt as the international postal service was not re-established for civilian mail at the time, he gave the letter to a neighbour, a lieutenant in the British army who was about to be redeployed to Germany. As luck would have it, this man was asked to attend a meeting with representatives of the other Allied Forces in Munich. He then decided to hand deliver the letter personally to the Lord Mayor and visited his office in the partially destroyed town hall. The Lord Mayor was unimpressed by his visitor and dismissed the request that he read the letter and take action. He asked the lieutenant to place the unopened letter on a pile of hundreds of similar letters and requests. The lieutenant was clearly not a man who took no for an answer: he was after all a member of the British army and carried a weapon. He leant across the desk and demanded again more forcefully that the Lord Mayor read the letter. This he eventually did, and much to the lieutenant's surprise, the Lord Mayor then called to his young secretary though the half-open door. No doubt he called in German, but they were words to the effect of: 'Sonja, your father is alive and he is looking for you.'

What took other families years and years of research – and in many cases did not produce the hoped-for result as family members had been murdered in the Holocaust or been killed in the hostilities – had only taken a few weeks in the case of Anton Hundsdorfer and his daughter. Father and daughter re-established contact and were able to communicate with each other again. Sonja got the rest of the day off to cope with the news and to write to her father and the lieutenant managed to get her letter to the UK.

Fanny and Anton decided to stay in the UK with their sons Peter and Ernie. However, they frequently visited Germany and Anton's daughter Sonja. Ernie and Peter spoke German as well as English. After his retirement, Ernie has become involved in telling his parents' story to younger generations in the UK and founded the Northern Holocaust Education Group. He is due to talk about his parents on Holocaust Memorial Day 2023 at Aberystwyth University.

Lia Lesser, Llanwrtyd Wells, 2022
(© Morris Brodie)

Lia Lesser's class at Czechoslovak School, Llanwrtyd Wells, 1940s (© Lia Lesser)

FINDING REFUGE ON YNYS MÔN:
LIA LESSER

When Lia Lesser was interviewed about her life, during one of the Kindertransport reunion events in the US, she told a very positive story. She admitted not being able to remember many details, and to having blanked out some of the most traumatic periods; however, her story is that of a woman at ease with herself.

Lia Lesser was born Lia Blum on 26 March 1931 in Teplice-Šanov, or Teplitz-Schönau to give it its German name. At that time, the town was located in the Sudetenland area of Czechoslovakia. Lia was the daughter of divorced parents: Ida Blum, who ran a haberdashery shop, and Paul (Pavel) Blum, a travelling salesman. The family was Jewish, as was about ten per cent of the local population at the time. However, they only attended synagogue on high holy days and Lia does not remember observing or celebrating any Jewish festivals at home. Lia lived with her mother and only saw her father at weekends. She was an only child but was surrounded by an extended family consisting of grandparents, one aunt and one uncle on her mother's side, and one aunt and one uncle on her father's side, plus two cousins. All her relatives would later be murdered in the Holocaust.

After the German Reich invaded Czechoslovakia and annexed the Sudetenland, Lia and her mother moved repeatedly to evade Nazi persecution. They stayed with a family of stonemasons in 1938, and she later remembered that she had a bad case of scarlet fever at that time and had lost all her hair. Their last place of residence was Prague in 1939; her mother had remarried, and they had their own flat. She had a new stepmother as well, as her father had also remarried, although Lia would forget about her until they met again after the war. Lia's mother told Lia that they would all emigrate to the US, but that Lia would have a stopover in the UK, and then her mother and stepfather would follow, and they would all three emigrate to the US together. Eight-year-old Lia believed that her stay in the UK would be a holiday. Therefore, she was not sad when she said goodbye to her mother at Prague station. Her father was very upset, and he did not want her to go.

In Wales, Florence Hall had felt that she wanted to help the persecuted and take in a Jewish refugee child. Lia describes in an interview how she was shown the transport list from Prague with Florence's name next to Lia's. This means that the placement had been arranged in advance. Lia later believed that Florence acted both as a guarantor and as a foster mother. Florence was a single woman and an English teacher by profession and lived on Ynys Môn. Florence's two brothers and her sister lived close by. Lia took a large suitcase on her journey with a lot of nice clothes that her mother had packed for her, a blue travel pillow that could be hung over her shoulder like a handbag, some Hebrew school books, some Czech story books, and a necklace with a pendant of Moses carrying law scrolls. The trip took two days: they left Prague station on 29 June 1939 and arrived in Liverpool Street Station on 1 July 1939. Lia remembered eating white bread sandwiches with jam at the Hoek of Holland and she thought they tasted lovely as she had never had white bread before (the bread in Central Europe was mainly rye bread and dark). She does not remember any children on the transport being upset.

When Florence picked up Lia, she was glad that her surname was at the beginning of the alphabet and that they got matched up quickly, as the train journey back to Ynys Môn was such a long way. Eight-year-old Lia felt strange but Florence knew German and spoke it to her, which must have been very reassuring. Most Kindertransportees could not communicate with their foster parents at all on arrival. On the long journey to North Wales, Lia got exhausted, and Florence was grateful to some Welsh sailors at

Crewe station who carried her from the train of the London line to the train of the North Wales line. They even sang lullabies in Welsh to Lia on the way to Amlwch, where Florence lived. Lia had no knowledge of the UK or Wales before she arrived.

Lia's story of her time with her foster mother in Wales is very positive. She called Florence Hall 'Mouse' as a term of endearment and had a very close relationship with her. Lia corresponded with both her birth father and birth mother, and they wrote back to her. In their letters they reminded her to be good, and to work hard at school and at learning English. Her parents also managed to correspond with her foster mother as they were all able to correspond in German. Lia remembered that she thought the landscape on Ynys Môn beautiful, even on the day she arrived, when she walked the last mile from Bull Bay to the bungalow in which her foster mother lived. When she opened the door of her new home, she saw a cat sitting on the table and thought to herself: 'It is going to be okay.' She liked cats and had had her own pet cat back in Czechoslovakia; the bungalow reminded her of home.

She did not know any English before she arrived in the UK. Initially, she went to a small primary school in Llangefni. Lia had no contact with other refugee children or Jewish children. However, the local people were very kind to her, and she had a lot of friends. She felt spoilt by the community. She went to Sunday School for social reasons, and she met other children there. Going to a Christian Sunday School did not upset her, as she had not really practised Judaism in Czechoslovakia. One of Florence Hall's sisters, Aunt Meg, gave her a book of Old Testament stories. At some point, Lia even asked whether she could get confirmed as other children were being confirmed. Florence told Lia that she did not want her to be confirmed and said that she needed to wait until she was an adult and then she could decide.

When Florence heard about the Czechoslovak boarding school in Llanwrtyd Wells, she decided to send Lia there because she had started to forget her Czech. (Incidentally, Lia forgot her German completely despite the fact that she initially spoke German with her foster mother. Lia later wondered whether this was for psychological reasons and that she wanted – whether consciously or subconsciously – to forget the language of the German aggressor.) Lia was very happy at the Czechoslovak boarding school. The community was tight and supportive, and Lia enjoyed sleeping in dormitories with the other girls, many of whom had had a similar refugee experience to her. The pupils at the school gave concerts, played table tennis, and produced their own school newspaper. Not all students were Jewish, but many were, and they had religious instruction each according to their beliefs. Lia remembered some very nice teachers. Lia always planned to return to her parents and to Czechoslovakia, but over the years her foster mother started to prepare her for the fact that this might not be possible by prefacing sentences about Lia's future life with, 'If your parents are still alive.' Lia still hoped that her birth mother would come to the UK at the end of the war to collect her despite the fact that she had not heard from her since 1939.

Lia stayed at the Czechoslovak boarding school from 1942 to 1945. In 1945, the school disbanded, as many pupils were united with parents or relatives, and some did move back to Czechoslovakia. However, this was not possible for Lia. At the end of the war, lists were published of those who were murdered in the Holocaust and these included the names of both of Lia's parents. Her father was murdered in Auschwitz, her mother and her other relatives in Theresienstadt. However, there was a subsequent surprise in the form of a letter from her stepmother, her father's second wife, which arrived after the end of the Second World War. Lia had no memories of this stepmother as she and Lia's father had not been married for very long before Lia left Prague, and life had felt very chaotic and confusing to the young girl at that time. However, her stepmother – who had also been deported to Theresienstadt, and then to Auschwitz, but survived – remembered Lia, traced her, and wrote to her. Florence Hall, with typical generosity, invited Lia's stepmother to come and stay in Amlwch with them. To Lia, it felt like meeting a complete stranger but she and her father's second wife came to know each other again and her stepmother went on to visit several more times.

Lia had moved back to Amlwch from Llanwrtyd in 1945 and she finished her education at the local grammar school, where Florence worked as a senior English teacher. Lia left school at sixteen to train as a nursery nurse, but her real desire was to go and train as a nurse in a hospital. Florence's sister, Aunt Meg, who was a health visitor, helped Lia realise this ambition and she began a nursing training course at Queen Elizabeth Hospital in Birmingham. Initially, Lia thought she might like to become a paediatric nurse, but she could not bear to see children suffer in pain, let alone die, so she trained as an adult nurse. Lia married a Jewish man with a Polish background in 1969 and they had two daughters. The family became part of their local Jewish community and attended synagogue. Lia kept in touch with Florence and Florence's relatives. She frequently took her daughters to visit the Halls on Ynys Môn and considered it like visiting relatives. Lia is still living in the Midlands at the time of writing. She attended a Tree Dedication Ceremony organised by the Association of Jewish Refugees on 28 April 2022, at the former location of the Czechoslovak school in Llanwrtyd Wells.

AJR Tree plaque, Llanwrtyd Wells, 2022
(© Morris Brodie)

Milena Grenfell-Baines, Llanwrtyd Wells, 2022
(© Morris Brodie)

'OUR WELSH HAVEN':
THE CZECHOSLOVAK STATE SCHOOL
IN LLANWRTYD WELLS

Lia Lesser was not the only former pupil to have very fond memories of the Czechoslovak State School in Llanwrtyd Wells. Vera Gissing and Ruth Hálová, who both also fled on a Kindertransport from Prague, had equally positive memories of their time at the school.

The Czechoslovak government-in-exile established a secondary school for refugees which was first located in Surrey and then at Hinton Hall in Shropshire. Eventually, it moved to the Abernant Lake Hotel in Llanwrtyd Wells, where it remained from 1943 to 1945. The boarding school had around 140 pupils, all of whom had fled to the UK. Some had arrived on a Kindertransport but others came with their parents, who ranged from those on workers' visas to members of the military or high officials and members of the Czechoslovak government-in-exile. Most pupils were from Jewish backgrounds but there were also Roman Catholics, Protestants and pupils with no religious affiliation.

The Czechoslovak State School was fully funded by the government-in-exile and Ruth Hálová, aged 17, was able to benefit from a free place there for the two years that the school was located in Wales. Ruth had initially arrived in London in 1939. She was 13 years old at the time and remembered being one of the older children on the transport who had to help with looking after the younger ones. Her foster parents lived in Birmingham, and were unable to pick her up in London, so she was put on a train to Birmingham together with some other Kindertransportees. Her foster parents were an older couple who ran a sweet shop. Looking back, Ruth felt that her foster parents and other members of the

119

local community tried to make settling in as easy as possible for her. When her foster parents saw how much she liked their pet dog, Peggy, they bought her other pets such as a kitten and a budgie. The butcher's helper from the store next door drove her around in the sidecar of his motorcycle. However, when her compulsory schooling came to an end when she was 14, her foster parents suggested that she might start working in their shop and establish a haberdashery section on the premises. She was not happy at the prospect of leaving school but her foster parents did not have the money to support her staying on.

Fortunately, she was able to gain the support of two wealthy Quakers and moved to a new foster family so that she was able to attend Rugby High School. Many Quakers were instrumental in the support networks for refugees, and especially in the organisation of the Kindertransport on a national and on a local level. They were part of local refugee committees and assisted both adult and child refugees. Ruth developed an interest in biology, and especially microbiology, having read a book on Louis Pasteur. Ruth left school at 16 with a leaving certificate, feeling she should find a job as soon as possible to stop her being a burden on her foster family's budget. Through one of her foster carers, she managed to get a job as an assistant in a laboratory at Hammersmith Hospital in London and planned to become a lab technician. However, the head of the laboratory thought that she should aim higher and fulfil her ambition of becoming a microbiologist, and so he wrote to the Czechoslovak government-in-exile to ask them to fund her studies. Ruth was not keen initially but when her boss visited the minister-in-exile and found out that a Czechoslovak exile school was just in the process of being opened in Wales, she was convinced to attend it and complete her Czech high school certificate there. Ruth left for Llanwrtyd Wells in the autumn of 1943 and enjoyed making many friends at the school. After what she later described as 'two beautiful years', she graduated from there in May 1945 at the end of the war. Miraculously, her mother had survived Theresienstadt and they were reunited on 25 August 1945 when Ruth travelled back to Czechoslovakia.

For these child refugees who would be returning to Czechoslovakia, it was obviously an advantage to speak fluent Czech. This was one of the central aims of the school. Another former pupil, Marilyn Yalom, later explained, 'It was clear that we all needed both to speak and to feel Czech, as the aim of the school was to prepare us to rebuild the republic devastated by the Nazis.'

Vera Gissing was very aware of the importance of language from an early age, even before she fled to the UK on a Kindertransport. In her memoirs, she described her father being spat at by a German officer who – after the German occupation of Prague – had requisitioned most of their flat (with the family restricted to a small part of it) and had demanded that from now on the whole family should speak German when in the presence of the German occupiers. Her father had refused, and the German officer's aggressive reaction and the humiliation of her father stuck in Vera's mind. Subsequently, her parents put her on a Kindertransport train and she was first resettled near Manchester. Her placement was successful, and Vera was keen to learn English from the beginning. When she had to move to a new family, as children were being evacuated out of urban centres, they proved equally supportive, and her English continued to improve. Nevertheless, despite this eagerness to learn English, she was also acutely aware of the danger of forgetting her Czech. When she met another young Czech refugee who had come to the UK some years before, without any contact with other Czech people, Vera was horrified by the girl's broken speech. She bluntly asked her, 'Why is your Czech so bad?' Learning that this was due to the other girl having no opportunity to practice, Vera vowed that she would never let this happen to herself.

Therefore, despite being very happy with both foster families she had lived with, Vera chose to go to the Czechoslovak State School, while it was at Hinton Hall in Shropshire. She subsequently moved with the school to Llanwrtyd Wells. In her memoirs, she described the locals as being somewhat bewildered by so many foreigners arriving in their small town:

'I shall never forget our arrival in the village of Llanwrtyd Wells, a small community which lies at the very heart of central Wales. We spilled out of the steam train at the tiny station and marched with our bags and cases along an unmade road. We could hardly believe our eyes when we saw our new home, for we had acquired not only a spacious modern building, but also several acres of rolling pastures with cows [...] Needless to say, the arrival of so many Czech youngsters (there were about 130 of us by then) caused quite a stir in the village and, at first, we were viewed with a mixture of curiosity and suspicion. Then one of our teachers had a brainwave; we organised a concert to which all the people of Llanwrtyd Wells were invited, and most of them came! The audience loved our national songs and dances, and when, at the end, all pupils of the school stood up and sang the Welsh national anthem in Welsh there was not a dry eye in the house.'

There seems to have been a particular affinity between the Czech child refugees and the local Welsh population. Former student Frank Schwelb also remembered 'with particular affection the Welsh people who welcomed' the children during a very difficult time for them. It was easier for Czech refugees to feel welcome in the UK than those from Germany or Austria, as their country was not the enemy against which the British Forces were fighting a war. The Czechoslovak people had not welcomed absorption by the National Socialist Reich as openly as had many Austrians. Despite the fact that refugees obviously had reasons why they had to flee the National Socialist German Reich, some British people did not properly understand the political situation. Some eyed all German speakers with suspicion. A few treated German and Austrian refugees from National Socialism with hostility regardless of their treatment by those in power. Czechoslovakians could more easily be identified as citizens of a country that had been invaded, and one which had, in fact, had a long history of being dominated by its larger neighbours. No doubt many Welsh people could identify with this situation. In turn, the children at the Czechoslovak school were appreciative of the Welsh language, most were at least already bilingual themselves, and they also understood what it was like to speak a language that was not spoken by many outside their own country.

The enduring affinity between Llanwrtyd Wells and the Czechoslovak people was confirmed many years after the end of the war and the closing of the school, when the town twinned with the Czech town of Český Krumlov in the early 1990s. Following a discussion with then Mayor of Llanwrtyd Wells, Bryan Watkins, at a reunion of the Czech School, this connection was initiated by Ruth Hálová.

The most well-known pupil of the school was not of secondary school age at the time, like Lia, Vera and Ruth but a primary school-aged boy. The Czechoslovak State School did not only educate secondary age pupils, it also had a boarding facility for younger pupils. The boy was Alfred Dubs, now Labour Life Peer Lord Alf Dubs, who also fled on a Kindertransport to the UK. He was only six years old at the time he fled Prague and only eight or nine years old when he was sent to the Czechoslovak State School by his parents during the war. In recent years, Alf has used his life story to support his campaign for a more generous refugee policy in the UK.

Alf left Prague for the UK on the Kindertransport in June 1939. In Prague, he had lived with his father, Hubert Dubs, whose family came from Northern Bohemia and who had a small cotton textile business, and his mother Bedřiška Ortner who was Austrian. After the Germans occupied Prague in March 1939, Alf's father, who was Jewish, left immediately for the UK. His non-Jewish mother was refused permission to leave. When she tried to talk to the German authorities, the Nazis threw her down the stairs. In June, Bedřiška put Alf on a Kindertransport train just with a knapsack of food for the journey – which he forgot to open and eat. Alf recalled later how his mother stood on the platform waving him off, surrounded by German soldiers in uniforms and wearing swastikas. Of course, for many of the parents waving their children off that day, it would be the last time they ever saw them. It took the train one-and-a-half days to get to the Dutch border and two days to get by train, ferry and then train again to Liverpool Street. Although the journey seemed interminably long to young Alf, it was not particularly traumatic. He remembered that some of the older children cheered after they had cleared the German border and were in the Netherlands. Six-year-old Alf did not understand the reasons for this. When the train from Harwich arrived at Liverpool Street station, Alf was in the enviable position of having his father waiting for him. He therefore only used a Kindertransport train for transport, and the visa-less entry into the UK. He was never fostered or needed a placement in care. Luckily, and somewhat unexpectedly, his mother made it to the UK on 31 August 1939, a couple of days before the government declared that Great Britain was at war with Germany. He was enrolled in a small school to learn English, and then a couple of years later, his parents sent him to the Czech school where he stayed until the end of the war. Alf's parents both spoke Czech and German, but his Jewish father spoke better German and his mother better Czech. They wanted Alf to learn Czech and the offer of a free education was also welcome.

Alf later said in an interview that fleeing Prague caused them to lose almost everything of the life they had had. The family left behind their home, almost all their possessions, and many members of their extended family and friends, most of whom were later murdered in the Holocaust. The family only had a handful of photos from their life in Prague, which they had been able to take with them. Alf continued to have a very positive attitude to his family's flight and resettlement in the UK. He felt that they were given a lot of opportunities in the UK to forge a new life and hope for a better future.

Alf Dubs certainly managed to make the most of these opportunities. After finishing school and studying at the London School of Economics, he initially worked as a government officer and in an accountancy firm before entering politics and becoming a Member of Parliament for Battersea South and later Battersea from 1979 to 1987. He was then appointed to a Life Peerage and sat in the House of Lords. He was Permanent Under-Secretary of State for Northern Ireland under Prime Minister Tony Blair from 1997 to 1999.

In this way, the refugee boy became a member of the UK government. For a long time, Dubs did not speak much about his refugee past. He recalled in an interview that he – like Renate Collins – only found out about the exact organisation of the Kindertransport from Prague in the late 1980s. But in recent years, Dubs has spoken more often about his early life. He mentioned his flight on a Kindertransport in a speech to rally support for an amendment to a bill about immigration. The Dubs amendment offered unaccompanied refugee children safe passage to the UK. He also founded the non-governmental organisation Safe Passage which continues to lobby for this cause.

Two photographs of Bea Green and family. Courtesy of Bea Green's personal archive and Association of Jewish Refugees (© AJR)

Bea Green as a girl. Courtesy of Bea Green's personal archive and Association of Jewish Refugees (© AJR)

EVACUATED TO WALES TWICE: BEA GREEN AT BRYN GWALIA HALL IN LLANGEDWYN AND UCL IN ABERYSTWYTH

Some of the younger Kindertransportees had little knowledge or memory of the country they left behind, and obviously also experienced Wales as very small children with little idea about the social or political context of the country that offered them refuge. This was different in the case of Bea Green, who was born Maria Beate Siegel into a Jewish family in 1925 in the Bogenhausen area of Munich, and left Germany in May 1939 aged 14. Her family was educated and wealthy, and both son and daughter were included in discussions about the rise of Nazism and the persecution of Jewish citizens. In later life, Bea talked openly about her experience of antisemitic persecution in Germany, her feelings about having to flee on her own, and how she felt when she was first resettled in England and then later in Wales.

In Germany, Bea was part of a well-to-do family: her father ran his own solicitors' practice and she had a nanny before she went to school. Because she was already 14 years old when she left Germany, she remembered the antisemitism and the Nazi persecution in Munich and Bavaria much more clearly than many child refugees. For example, she experienced early antisemitic incidents in school in 1932 when a teacher made hateful remarks about money and Jewish children. The following year, on 10 March 1933, Bea had been at home alone in the flat when her father came home injured after a violent antisemitic attack. That was the day on which she first really felt fear in the realisation that something was going on that her parents did not want her to know about. Her father had been attacked because he acted on behalf of a Jewish client whose store had been vandalised. When he tried to report this crime to the police, he was attacked by Nazis in the building of the police headquarters. He was beaten up, his trouser legs were cut off, and the thugs forced him to wear a sign saying, 'I will not ask for protection from the police again' before parading him around Munich to humiliate him. A photo of this incident went around the world – a foreign correspondent had witnessed what had happened and had taken a picture. The picture was used to demonstrate the deteriorating situation in Germany and illustrated reports in many international newspapers, including the front page of *The Washington Times*.

Bea was one of five Jewish children in her grammar school class of 35 and, while there seemed to be no overt antisemitism like that she had experienced in primary school, the five girls nonetheless remained somehow separate from the rest of the class. But she did not mind much as she was friendly with the other Jewish girls. After 1938, Bea was no longer allowed to go to the grammar school and was instead sent to a Jewish cookery school, starting there in January 1939. She remembered in an interview: 'You had to be 16 to attend the cookery school and I was only 13, but my mother just ignored this and said I was 16. I was accepted into the cookery school and I loved it.'

Despite the early violent attack on her father, the family was very reluctant to leave Germany. Her father initially felt defiant and wanted to stay in Germany as he did not think the Nazis should have the power to turf him out. Later, Mr Siegel felt that he could not consider giving up his career. As a German lawyer, he was only really qualified to practise in Germany. However, by 1937, he wanted to leave Germany but could not find anywhere to go. Some relatives had gone to Palestine, but Michael and his family could not get an entry visa. He even invested in a plot of land in Palestine, but the agent pocketed the money. Applying for a permit to enter the UK did not appeal as he did not want to work as a butler, and there seemed to be no other avenues open to him. Instead, he worked on his rabbinic knowledge and organised the departure of his son and daughter for the UK.

Bea never knew who paid her guarantee of £50 for UK entry. She was offered a foster placement by a Mrs Williams, who was a Liberal, with an explicit anti-Nazi stance. Mrs Williams was very much against appeasement and felt that she could help her cause by assisting the victims of Nazi oppression. She had already agreed to take a girl from Hamburg, and maybe thought that it would be easier to foster two girls as they then would have company. Mrs Williams was from a wealthy family and lived in Brasted Hall, near Sevenoaks in Kent. In this way, Bea moved from a well-off family to an extremely well-off one.

A list dated May 1939 details all the items that Bea brought to the UK. The list was extensive and, in the end, she brought three suitcases and one laundry sack with her. This was against the regulations, which allowed children on the Kindertransport to bring only one suitcase and one small bag, an amount they could carry by themselves. Clearly Bea's mother felt this was insufficient and somehow got away with bending the rules. Bea's suitcases included an extensive wardrobe and the sack included her dowry, which consisted of monogrammed sheets and the like. She also brought an accordion with her.

The Kindertransport trains from Munich left at midnight. Many have interpreted this timing as a surreptitious attempt to hide the heartbreaking farewells. The general German population was prevented from seeing what was going on. Bea later remembered that she had not felt sad until that moment, even though all her friends and her parents managed to come to the station to see her off. When she saw her mother pull out a handkerchief and cry, emotion hit her, but because she had been asked to look after a little girl, she tried not to cry and risk upsetting her. Bea experienced many different emotions during her journey to the UK. Kindertransport refugees were only allowed to bring 10 Marks out of Germany. But her mother had put another 10 Marks into her sandwich. This worried Bea greatly. She was scared that the border police would investigate her sandwich and find the money. However, she also experienced relief and happiness after crossing the border safely, when some Dutch women entered the train and gave the children orange juice and white bread and butter. Bea later claimed that nothing in her whole life had ever tasted so good.

In London, Bea was picked up by Mrs Williams's daughter, Estelle, in a chauffeur-driven Mercedes. She spent the next two nights with her in inner London and then they were driven to Bea's new home at Brasted Hall, where she met the other foster girl and Mrs Williams. Bea was addressed as 'Miss' by the housekeeper and other domestic staff at the Hall and treated very well. Both girls were sent to a small local private school where Bea got on well. Unfortunately, Mrs Williams died in January 1940 but she left a trust fund for the benefit of both refugee girls. Mrs Williams's son, Colonel Ainslie Williams, was put in charge of this fund and the girls, and he supported them until they finished their education.

The school in Sevenoaks was bombed and then evacuated to Wales. The headteachers of the school were Welsh and they had already rented a property near Welshpool. Although Bea enjoyed being at the school and was successful there, the complete immersion in British middle-class culture, with little by way of explanation, did sometimes cause her to struggle. For example, she later described her experience of being made to play cricket one day: 'They strapped funny things to my legs and gave me a wooden thing and told me to go out to hit the ball.' The terminology was strange and incomprehensible. 'What,' she wondered, 'did it mean to be out for a duck?' However, despite this initial bewilderment, Bea did take to cricket and in time was even asked to play for the boys' team. She was also criticised for her table manners; no one had the awareness to imagine that the rules might be different in Germany. Bea felt that she could neither ask nor complain about such matters as that would be letting her parents down. Astonishingly, she later remembered being more scared that she might be picked on for being a refugee in the UK, than for being a Jew in Germany.

When the school was evacuated, most pupils went home to live with their parents and only 12 or 13 children went to Wales with the headmistress. The first location for the school turned out to be haunted, and the children and their teacher then moved to Bryn Gwalia Hall. The headmistress could only teach geometry and French, so the rest of the subjects were taught from textbooks and by correspondence with some of the school's teachers who had remained in London. Bea played an important role in the school, looking after younger pupils and going shopping. She got on well with the Welsh locals she met on her shopping trips and felt that they liked her: 'The Welsh adored me in principle because I wasn't English.'

In 1941, Bea managed to pass her school certificate. Again, no one had explained the system to her, and she had to ask the headmistress what receiving a school certificate actually meant. The head explained that it entitled her to go to university. However overnight, on her 16th birthday on 14 March 1941, Bea became an enemy alien. This felt very strange to her:

> 'You see to me I wasn't a refugee, to me I'd come here and what they thought was their problem. When I went to this police station ... I suppose it was fortunate that it was in Wales because they made light of it. I just knew it hit people ... and again it was something that happened like bad weather ... you know you just took it ... and I had this card ... the Welsh police were rather sweet. You know I don't think it impinged a lot. What impinged was something much deeper that I was coping with, by saying to myself "I'll show them who I am".'

Meantime, the situation of Bea's parents had changed. At first, following her departure, they had remained in Munich, having lost their second home in rural Bavaria, and no longer being allowed to work. Their bank accounts were frozen, and their desperate attempts to find a country they could flee to had been unsuccessful. They had started taking Spanish lessons from a Peruvian student, but for a long time did not discuss any personal matters with him. When they finally did, it turned out that their tutor was the nephew of the Peruvian Minister for the Interior, who was prepared to arrange emigration for them. They were asked how many visas they wanted (they just said two!) and were able to pick them up a few weeks later. Their bank account was unblocked following diplomatic intervention and they were able to buy tickets for travel. Their complicated journey took them east from Berlin, via the Trans-Siberian Railway to Manchuria, and then on to Japan, from where they were able to take a ship to Peru. During the course of their journey, Bea's parents sent a telegram from Irkutsk to a family contact in London. It simply stated, 'Travelling to Peru. Inform children.' When this message reached Bea at Bryn Gwalia Hall in Powys, she was overwhelmed with emotion. She later described this as 'the most wonderful feeling of relief'.

The five refugee children who attended the school and lived at Bryn Gwalia Hall had to do a lot of chores and even supervised younger students. Bea later felt that the school had been run almost like a commune. They had a lot of work with housework, supervising younger pupils and doing their own schoolwork. The refugee girls had to do all this while worrying about their families. The Refugee Children's Committee offered little support. Bea does not remember anyone visiting the girls to check up on them and nor was there any religious instruction available to them in the 'middle of Mid-Wales'.

Bea enjoyed more good fortune on the financial front as Ainslie Williams continued to support her. When she informed him that she had passed her school certificate and that this meant she might be able to go to university, there was little reaction. A few weeks later, Williams asked her if she wanted to go to university but gave little detail on how this might be achieved. She answered in the affirmative and again heard nothing more. However, behind the scenes, Colonel Williams was not being idle. Eventually, and by which point she had begun attending a secretarial college, she was informed that three universities were willing to take her. Oxford was willing to admit her, but she would have to wait a year as she was still under 18. Reading and University College London (UCL) were also willing to take her and would let her start immediately. As she had never heard of Reading but obviously knew of London, she decided to accept a place at UCL. By October 1942, however, UCL had been evacuated to Aberystwyth and so Bea made her way to Wales for a second time. She had to catch up in Latin which had not been taught in her old school, but after two months she successfully passed her Latin exam.

Bea made some friends and generally enjoyed her time in Aberystwyth very much. She studied German, became a member of the German Society and the captain of the rowing club, rowing weekly in the sea. She made a best friend, and moved out of her boarding house, and in with the friend. They stayed friends for the rest of their lives. There were some negative experiences as well: she did encounter antisemitic attitudes in a fellow student. There were only six or seven students studying German in her year, and one of them, Stan Price, had been an enthusiastic Nazi and had worked for the Arbeitsdienst before the war. The Arbeitsdienst was the National Socialist labour agency set up to help mitigate the effects of unemployment on the German economy by militarising the workforce and indoctrinating it with Nazi ideology. Price only returned to the UK when war broke out. In the UK, despite his apparent adherence to National Socialist ideology, he had joined the army but injured himself in training, and was invalided out of the Forces. This somehow made him feel dissatisfied with the British, and it reignited his enthusiasm for Nazi ideology. He talked about the superiority of the master race and made antisemitic remarks. Bea felt that it was impossible to argue with him and when she pointed out that she was Jewish, he said that he 'did not mean her' and that 'she was all right'.

After one such altercation, Bea found herself sitting on the pebbles on the beach in Aberystwyth and feeling very depressed. She felt that things were repeating themselves, and that what she had been trying to get away from was catching up with her. Fortunately, this did not happen often. Retrospectively, Bea felt that at the time she simply did not have the mental reserves to deal with such bullying, and that she would have been able to deal with it more effectively later in her life when she'd had more time to recover from the trauma of the Nazi period.

Bea stayed in Aberystwyth for two years before her university department relocated back to London in 1944, where she finished her degree. Bea felt that in London her UCL department lost some of the feeling of unity that it had had in Aberystwyth, where everything was much smaller and closer and they had been able to join in activities with University College Wales students.

In 1947, Bea's brother contracted polio and their parents scraped all their money together so that Mrs Siegel could travel to the UK from Peru. It was a very strange experience for Bea to meet her mother again. She wasn't the daughter she had been when they last saw each other, and her mother had obviously changed as well.

Kindertransportees who were reunited with their parents after the end of the Second World War are often considered the lucky ones; however, re-establishing a relationship between refugee children and their parents was not easy. There were cases where the challenges thrown up by separation were not overcome successfully and the parent-child relationship was never restored. Fortunately, this was not the case here and the different members of the Siegel family established new bonds.

After Bea's first marriage broke down, she lived with her parents in Peru for two years between the ages of 27 to 29. Her father managed to re-establish a career for himself as a lawyer fighting for compensation for German Jews who had fled to South America. He was even awarded the Bundesverdienstkreuz, the highest honour the Federal Republic of Germany can bestow on an individual, for his efforts. When he submitted the list of items that he personally had lost when his solicitors' practice was taken over by the Nazis, the judge in charge of his case asked him whether he had forgotten anything. When Siegel replied that he did not think so, the judge told him that he had forgotten to claim compensation for his green sofa. The judge had once been one of Michael Siegel's pupils and still remembered him. What might have been a painful occasion was transformed by this personal reconnection and the Siegel family were able to re-establish a positive relationship with their birth country again. Bea returned from Peru to live in London, where she became a teacher and an author and lives today.

Susi Bechöfer speaking to schoolchildren on behalf
of the Holocaust Educational Trust
(© Holocaust Educational Trust)

RECLAIMING CONTROL OVER HER LIFE AND HER STORY: SUSI BECHHÖFER IN CARDIFF AND BEYOND

In contrast to the experiences of Lia Lesser and Bea Green, the story of three-year-old twins Lotte and Susi Bechhöfer is one of the most disturbing and complicated of all Kindertransport stories. Their parents' relationship and their start in life was already beset by difficulties before the war broke out.

The twins' mother, Rosa Bechhöfer, was born the twelfth child in a Jewish family of 13 children. Both her parents died before she was eight years old. She was raised by her siblings and worked in one of her sister's shoe shops. By the mid-1930s, some of her family had already managed to emigrate to the US, but she had not been so lucky. When she met Otto Hald, she was 37 and he was 28 but, more importantly, she was Jewish and he was considered Aryan. Almost from the start their relationship was considered illegal as the Nuremberg Laws were in the process of being passed to 'preserve the purity of German blood and honour' by forbidding sexual relationships between Jews and non-Jews. Rosa was surprised when she fell pregnant as she had thought that she might already be too old to have children. At first Otto was pleased, but circumstances were overwhelmingly against them sharing a happy future together as the regime continued to enact increasingly antisemitic measures. Rosa moved away from the area of Munich where she had first met Otto to a Jewish zone to live with her sister and brother-in-law. They helped her and funded her stay in the maternity hospital.

Lotte and Susi were born on 17 May 1936. Both babies were healthy but, because they were twins, they were small and Rosa took some time to recover from the birth. After a few days, she settled into the rhythm of feeding, changing, and settling Lotte and Susi and they all stayed at the hospital for three months. Rosa's sister visited her and passed on the occasional message to Otto. He did not dare to visit, and it became clear that Rosa would have to bring up the children without the support of a father. She also informed those family members who had already fled to the US of the twins' birth, but this news was met with no positive response, as being an unmarried mother was an affront to their ideas of religion and morality. After about three months, the twins were placed in a Jewish orphanage, the Antonienheim in Munich, and Rosa started working as a cook and housekeeper for several Jewish families in the city. Rosa visited the twins on her free Sundays. During the rest of the time, they were cared for by the staff and the older children of the orphanage. Because they were so tiny, and because they were twins, they received a lot of attention from all at the orphanage.

Social worker Alice Bendix was the director of the orphanage. An energetic and well-organised woman, she was extremely keen that her charges should not attract any undue attention and therefore they were told to behave impeccably in public all the time. These worries were not unfounded. Jewish orphanages were visible and vulnerable to antisemitic mobs. This was known to the leaders of the Jewish communities, and they were keen to place children from children's homes on the earliest Kindertransport trains. Alice Bendix tried to get a place for the twins. Initially, Rosa was completely taken aback by the suggestion that her children should be sent abroad. She did not want to give up them up, even though she could not care for them full-time. However, before long Rosa realised that it was too dangerous for her children to stay in Germany, and she consented to them leaving Munich on a Kindertransport to the UK.

A foster placement for the twins was arranged in advance of their departure. Fred Legge, a Baptist minister from Cardiff, and his wife Audrey, had agreed to provide a home for Lotte and Susi Bechhöfer. The Legges had not been able to have biological children, and this was something that Fred especially found very difficult to live with. Although the placements for all the Kindertransport refugees were fostering arrangements, a small number of the foster parents in the UK either chose to ignore that it was not planned for them to adopt the children or the British organising committees failed to communicate this fact to them. Some foster parents therefore made no effort to help these young refugees remember their birth parents or their home country. Religion was also a contentious matter as there were different opinions about the requirement for religious observance among the organisers of the Kindertransport. Some believed that Jewish children should only be placed with Jewish foster families, but there were just not enough Jewish foster families in the UK to accommodate those arriving. (The Jewish population in the UK in 1933 was just 300,000 or around 0.65 per cent of the whole population.) Others believed that the only thing that mattered was to save the child's life and there was no need to make an effort to maintain their religion.

Of course, we must acknowledge that common views on what is best for the welfare of a child have changed drastically over the last 80 years. Some foster parents might have genuinely believed that it would be less painful and better for the child refugee to forget their past. However, in the case of Fred Legge, it seems that his behaviour, including the decision to bring the girls up as Baptists, was driven by a rather selfish wish that everyone should think he was the biological father of the twins, rather than any kind but misguided attempt to make things less painful for the children.

The twins arrived at Liverpool Street Station on 18 May 1939, the day after their third birthday. The journey must have been extremely bewildering for them as they had not left the orphanage since they'd arrived as three-month-old babies. Later they would remember their arrival at the home of Fred and Audrey as traumatic. Lotte and Susi had no way of communicating with their foster parents, and to make things extra confusing for them, their names were immediately changed by the Legges to Eunice Mary and Grace

Elizabeth Legge, respectively. Fred tried to pretend that the twins were his birth children and got very annoyed if anyone asked about their origin.

However, as was common in the 1930s, this did not mean that he saw himself as their principal carer. He left the day-to-day care of the twins to his wife. Initially this involved extra care and the administration of vitamins and cod liver oil as their GP had detected malnutrition, with a danger of developing rickets. Caring for twin toddlers with health concerns was not easy and kept Audrey from pursuing her church interests and seeing her friends, which frustrated her. The Legges had very regimented ideas about child rearing and the girls were expected to follow a rigid schedule which included helping with household chores from a very young age. However, their life was not without leisure pursuits. There are photos of them, labelled 'on holiday', which show them feeding the ducks in a park and another one of them together with Audrey, labelled 'Pen-y-bryn, Cardiff'.

By the time the twins started school at a local primary, the Second World War was dominating most people's thoughts and the girls were teased for being German. This upset Fred greatly, but it has been suggested that this was mainly because he wanted the children to be seen as his own and, furthermore, he did not want them to be reminded of their past. He immediately removed Susi and Lotte from the local school and sent them instead to a small private school in Llandaff called Elm Tree House.

Unfortunately, another serious problem arose. Lotte became very unwell when she was seven. She fell behind with her schoolwork, started walking in an unusual way, and her character appeared to change. Initially the Legges thought that she was just behaving badly but then they started consulting doctors. Eventually, after numerous hospital visits, Lotte was diagnosed with a brain tumour. The tumour was removed surgically, but from then on until her death, aged 35, Lotte needed constant care. This whole traumatic experience affected Susi negatively as well. The Legges also found the situation difficult; in addition they were experiencing problems in their professional life. Fred was a minister in the Baptist Church in Wales but his main duties were lecturing and educating rather than looking after a congregation. Complaints were made against the Reverend Legge and there were suggestions that he might not be suitable as a lecturer. Fred was still unable to acknowledge the twins' origins and, apparently, used to tell Susi, 'You are Grace Elizabeth Legge, and you are mine.'

The Legges were also very ambitious, Susi remembered that they were always plotting their next move, both regarding their accommodation or their profession. For example, from their house in Cardiff, they had moved to a manse in Penarth. Susi spent a lot of time on her own here, as she was not allowed friends or at least not allowed to bring anyone back home. Therefore, while she was left with some fond memories of the blossoming rhododendrons and the rose garden, she had none of actually being happy with other people. The denial of her true origins, the Legges' controlling behaviour and the illness of her sister all weighed heavily on her. At some point she was sent away to boarding school which was a relief to her – and possibly her foster parents – and she enjoyed her time there.

Only after years and years, was Susi able to speak fully about what happened during her childhood. Fred Legge was not only very controlling, he also sexually abused his foster daughter. When she was back from boarding school, she would have to spend hours locked away with Fred in his study, and he would abuse her and the same would happen in her bedroom at night. Susi felt that Fred had complete control over her life, and she only managed to survive the repeated trauma by disassociating herself from these events.

But the trauma would have a habit of emerging at unexpected moments and led to mental health problems. In 1952, when Grace Elizabeth Legge, as she was then called, was 16 years old and about to sit her O levels at school, she was informed by her teacher that she needed to sit the examinations under her birth name Susi Bechhöfer. This reminded her of the unresolved questions regarding

141

her history and led to a breakdown and the inability to continue with the examinations. Although Susi eventually managed to overcome the mental health problems that were triggered on that day and pass her exams, before going on to qualify as a nurse, it remained a traumatic memory. Susi led an outwardly successful life; besides her nursing career, she found a partner and got married, although Fred tried to stop her from doing so repeatedly. The couple had a son and for a long time Susi's past stayed in the past. However, throughout her 30s and 40s, the buried trauma affected her mental and physical health. Susi suffered from depression and from something we would now probably call burnout, especially in relation to her stressful work as a nurse.

One day she heard a radio programme in which the Kindertransport was discussed – the programme featured Berta Leverton, also a former child refugee who had fled on a Kindertransport. In the late 1980s, Leverton was instrumental in organising the first reunion of those who had fled to the UK in this way. Listening in, Susi realised that she must be one such child and she contacted other Kindertransport refugees and for the first time started to understand how the scheme had been organised and that there were about 10,000 others who had been part of this rescue mission, many of whom had also lost their parents. Subsequently, Susi spent years researching her past and eventually discovered that he mother had been deported to Auschwitz and murdered there in 1943. She also found out she had surviving relatives in the US and even met a half-sister on her biological father's side. Her story attracted public attention and she wrote a memoir together with Jeremy Jacobs, which was published in 1996. There was also a TV documentary. When I met Susi, she was not very happy about either the memoir or the documentary. She felt that her co-author had dominated the memoir writing process and used her material in an unethical way. The TV documentary did not mention the sexual abuse as no doubt it was felt that this would be too controversial and potentially defamatory if contested.

Sadly, this was not to be the last time that Susi was left feeling that others had taken control of her story. Incidents from her life as told in the documentary and her memoir, such as being told to sit her exam under her birth name, were used by the German writer, W G Sebald in his novel *Austerlitz*. Sebald was an academic as well as a writer of fiction and Germany's recent past was one of his main themes. He used parts of Susi's story as a blueprint for the main character of the novel, Jacques Austerlitz, a five-year-old from Prague who comes to the UK on a Kindertransport. The Kindertransport experience in *Austerlitz* is represented as a mark of pain and there are clear parallels between the things that happened to Susi and how that Kindertransport experience is narrated in *Austerlitz*. Sebald had always talked publicly about his conviction that any form of usurpation of Jewish history and suffering by non-Jewish (and especially by a German) writer was problematic and morally wrong, but this is exactly what he seemed to have done himself in this case. When Susi asked him about the matter, Sebald admitted that her story had inspired his novel, but he never added an acknowledgement to his published work upsetting Susi greatly. *Austerlitz* was published in 2001 and Sebald died the same year in a car crash.

Susi's story of fleeing from Nazi Germany to Wales as a very young child refugee is undoubtedly one of the more traumatic ones. There are complicated reasons for this trauma, which does not lie only in Nazi persecution and the murder of Susi's family, or in the UK government's decision to waive visa restrictions for child refugees while hindering their parents from accompanying those children. In this case, the trauma was further compounded by the criminal and abusive behaviour of someone who should have been caring and supportive, and by the lack of oversight by the authorities once the children had arrived in the UK and been allocated to foster carers. It is important to tell this story, which Susi fought so long to gain control over. As we have seen elsewhere in this book, many Welsh men and women went to great lengths to help refugees from

Nazism. Many offered their homes and families as foster placements to child refugees, but some abused their power over the vulnerable. Many child refugees, such as Lia Lesser and Renate Collins, felt the warmth and the love of their foster parents, but others suffered further trauma. We must acknowledge that such things happened since this is also a part of the history of refugees from National Socialism in Wales. Susi died in 2018 but published another autobiographically inspired text with the title *Rosa* prior to her death.

Wolfgang Dienemann
(as he was then) in 1936
– first day at school
(© Rachel Dieneman)

William Dieneman meeting
Prince Charles at the official
opening of Hugh Owen Library
(© Rachel Dieneman)

ESTABLISHING A CAREER AT UNIVERSITY COLLEGE WALES ABERYSTWYTH: WILLIAM DIENEMAN

William Dieneman came on a Kindertransport to the UK, but first lived in England and only moved to Wales as an adult. After his appointment as university librarian at Aberystwyth he lived on the west coast of Wales until his death in 2018. William was born Wolfgang Dienemann into a non-practising Jewish family in Cottbus on 6 December 1929. His sister Ursula had been born five years earlier, and the family first lived in Cottbus and later in Berlin. Their father had studied law and worked initially as a Landgerichtsrat, a county court judge. He had volunteered in the First World War and had been awarded the Iron Cross, First and Second Class, as a lieutenant in the artillery. He was promoted to judge at the Kammergerichts, the Appelate Court in the Schöneberg district of Berlin in 1930. After the Nazis rose to power, they immediately introduced laws and policies to drive Jewish people out of the professions, and especially out of the civil service. Because William's father had served at the front for Germany, he was initially only demoted to the county court level. However, in 1935, he was dismissed and had to try and make a living as a lawyer while only being allowed to represent Jewish clients.

William/Wolfgang was enrolled in the Jewish primary school in Schöneberg in 1936, and there are photos showing him with the customary large cone in his arms on his first day of school. This German tradition of giving children a cardboard cone filled with sweets and presents on their first day of school continues to this day. The school was attached to the synagogue, the Prinzregentensynagoge. William later remembered making his way to school all on his own as there was little traffic in those days. He also remembered playing on the Bayrische Platz when not in school and feeding the ducks in the Stadtpark with his grandfather. The family led an ordinary middle-class life in Berlin. William was cared for by a nanny and remembered holidays in the Harz mountains and in Denmark.

Beyond this handful of pleasant memories, however, Dieneman only remembered extraordinary occurrences such as the time he got his foot stuck between the underground train and the platform but fortunately he was freed before the train started moving. Another such extraordinary day was the morning of 10 November 1938, the day after the November Pogrom. Somewhat surprisingly, given what had just happened, William's parents sent him to school and William, aged eight, later remembered being quite happy to find that the school had burnt down (as it was attached to the synagogue) and there would be no lessons that day. He was told to go back home, but he did not do so. He went to the house of a friend, a little girl the same age as him, and played outside with her for the whole day. Of course, his parents were extremely worried as they did not know where he had gone, or whether something had happened to him. When he finally came home, they were so relieved they did not tell him off. Many Kindertransportees mentioned the November Pogrom and what they did on the day after in their later recollections of their wartime experience. The pogrom was clearly a turning point in many families' decision-making processes regarding emigration. After Kristallnacht, the urgency of the situation became completely clear to many, and this led to parents deciding to send their children abroad despite not being able to accompany them on the journey.

This was also a time of mass arrests. When the Gestapo came to the door of the Dienemann flat, Ursula truthfully told them that their father had not come home from work yet. The plain-clothes Gestapo came back later and arrested William's father, who was incarcerated in Sachsenhausen concentration camp. William remembered the strange transition from being normal citizens to outcasts. Their neighbours in Berlin, the Von Klodts, were Nazis. However, after William's father was arrested, Mr Von Klodt came round with a bunch of flowers expressing his sympathy. Dienemann senior wrote a postcard from Sachsenhausen urging William's mother to get the children out of Germany as quickly as possible. This must have meant that she put both Ursula and William on a waiting list for a Kindertransport to the UK. After the school and the synagogue burnt down, William did not go out anymore. William's father was released from Sachsenhausen after six weeks, but he was in a bad state of health having been hit with batons. He had to have an ear operation before leaving Berlin.

William's father was a member of the Association of Jewish Ex-Servicemen (AJEX) in Germany which had connections to its sister organisation in the UK. Through this connection he knew someone who helped to find a guardian for the children, possibly also a guarantor, or maybe the AJEX paid the compulsory guarantees of £50. Whichever way it was, he successfully got his children on the Kindertransport. William and Ursula did not come to the UK on the usual train and ferry route via the Hoek of Holland and Harwich. They took a train to Hamburg and travelled on the SS Manhattan to Southampton arriving in the UK on 16 January 1939.

After Ursula's and William's arrival in England, they first stayed with a Jewish family in Bristol who had a large furniture store. As has been discussed, due to the haste with which arrangements had to be made, little thought was given to the question of compatibility between refugees and hosts. Ursula and William's foster family was culturally completely different from the Dienemann family. This family were Orthodox Jews from an East European background. William did not feel at home: 'I felt that the family resented these well-dressed, assimilated children from Berlin coming into their house.' In other cases, this sort of situation led to more than resentment and could result in the foster parent-child relationship breaking down. Some observant Jewish foster parents felt tricked as they had expected an observant Jewish child but instead had been matched with a child with no idea of Jewish traditions at all. William soon left this foster family and was given a free place at the Avondale Prep Boarding School in Bristol during term time. He thus received a very good education. A number of boarding schools generously provided such free places.

The Dienemann parents were able to get away from Germany in May 1939. They had a transit visa to Great Britain and were supposed to emigrate to the US within a year. They were put up by a wealthy brewery heiress, Doris Wethered, in a house outside Bristol. It was there that William's father was finally able to recuperate fully from his mistreatment. In 1940, however, he was interned on the Isle of Man as an enemy alien, and William's mother became a domestic servant in Oxford. William's father was not able to cope with being interned, especially after his previous experiences in Sachsenhausen. He felt unfairly treated, and that the world was against him. His physical and mental health declined dramatically.

Avondale School closed during the war and William was evacuated to Oxford where he went to Oxford High School. His school fees were paid by the Oxford Refugee Committee and he stayed with different foster families. Later, he remembered feeling quite uncomfortable at this school at times: both for being German and for being Jewish. He did not want to be German, and there was a certain degree of antisemitism at the school. What William found particularly difficult was that there was no family home. Even though all four family members had managed to flee to the UK, they never managed to live as a family again. William saw his sister only rarely and had to stay with foster families as his parents were not able to afford a home where he could live with them permanently.

There was a big refugee community in Oxford; they had a *Reformgemeinde* where William had his bar mitzvah. William later expressed that this was the last time in his life when he felt that he had a real connection with Jewish life. After receiving his school certificate (while living with yet another family, the Bruckers), William sat the entrance scholarship for Jesus College, Oxford, but did not pass. This was largely due to the fact that he got very ill and ended up in hospital for two months with rheumatic fever. On his recovery, William was able to get a job at Christ Church Library as a junior clerk and the dean of Christ Church college made sure that he attended lectures. It was decided that it might be too difficult for him to read Classics, so he studied German and French and graduated in 1951 from Christ Church, Oxford. Following on from his degree, he went to the School of Librarianship at UCL; again, his fees were paid by a charity.

Before settling in Aberystwyth, William gathered experience in a number of different positions. After he qualified as a librarian, he worked at the Commonwealth Forestry Institute in Oxford for two or three years. At this time, his parents finally obtained a flat together in Oxford. William's father worked in the accounts department of the local Co-op until his retirement and received a pension from the German government, which helped him both financially and psychologically. After 1945, the Federal Republic of Germany paid reparations to the victims of Nazi persecution – although the victims had to file a claim and it was not an easy process. Those who could prove that they would have been entitled to pensions had they not been persecuted, generally received them and this was clearly the case for William's father.

In 1954, William applied to become a librarian in Nigeria, at Ibadan University, and got the job. This was very exciting for 24-year-old William, and he worked in Nigeria for seven years. He enjoyed this very much as he had the money and the opportunity to travel to neighbouring countries whilst he was there. He then successfully applied for a library job at Trinity College Dublin (TCD) in 1962.

In Dublin, he met his future wife, Marisa, the daughter of an American diplomat. As she was under 21 and her parents did not give her permission to marry William, the couple eloped and were married in England in 1964. Back in Dublin, William worked his way up to deputy librarian at TCD. Marisa's parents had been posted to Tokyo, and later on their return, there was a reconciliation in Dublin. William and Marisa's daughter Rachel was born in 1967.

In 1970, William became college librarian at University College Wales, Aberystwyth, and the family moved to Wales. They lived in a beautiful house on Penglais Hill, where they enjoyed chamber music (William) and collecting ceramics (Marisa). They were well respected professionally and became part of the Aberystwyth community despite, or maybe because of, their backgrounds: a German Jewish refugee who had worked in Nigeria and Ireland, and an American diplomat's daughter of Japanese descent who had studied in Ireland. William was a member of the Association of Jewish Refugees and attended a Kindertransport reunion. There was no Jewish community in Aberystwyth for him to connect with. He did, however, lead a German reading group. I met William soon after I arrived in Aberystwyth. When one of his neighbours, the late David Trotter, Professor of French and Head of the Modern Languages Department, pointed out to me that William had escaped from Berlin on a Kindertransport, I visited William and Marisa and wrote down his story. This shows that his past was not unknown in Aberystwyth. However, when I invited him to give a talk at the University in 2012, the local newspaper, the *Cambrian News*, headlined an article about the talk as 'Jewish man who escaped Nazis tells his story'. This caused some consternation for William as he felt outed in public. (William explained to me that he thought that not many members of the local community knew he was Jewish.) He took it with good grace, though. His talk was extremely well attended with an audience of over 120 people.

After William retired from the library in 1995, he worked as a volunteer advisor for the Citizens Advice Bureau (Citizens Advice Cymru) and Age Concern (Age Cymru). He and Marisa regularly attended concerts and enjoyed lunch at the Aberystwyth Arts Centre. William was also an engaged member of his

Neighbourhood Watch scheme. During the years I visited him, he enjoyed talking most about his early life and about present-day university life; latterly he was affected by dementia. He died in 2018 and is survived by his daughter Rachel, who still lives near Aberystwyth.

Arieh Handler's wedding at Gwrych Castle (© Aviv Handler)

'WE WERE EXCITED ABOUT LIVING IN A CASTLE': TEENAGE REFUGEES AT GWRYCH AND LLANDOUGH CASTLES

In the late 1930s, many Continental Jewish refugees were actively looking to flee to the UK, however, there were more who wanted to resettle in other parts of the world, including Palestine. To make Aliyah – to return to the Jewish homeland in order to assist in creating a Jewish state – was the aim of many Jews whether they were members of a Zionist organisation or not. An increasing number had managed to make this move in the 1920s and early 1930s. However, the UK government, which was administering Palestine on behalf of the League of Nations, had been facing understandable challenges from the Arab population in the territory and consequently placed restrictions on Jewish immigration to the area from the German Reich. It was therefore becoming increasingly impossible for the Youth Aliyah movement to get permission to organise activities within Palestine and train young people to live in kibbutzim. Training young people in Britain was seen as an alternative, as many believed that once they were in Britain they might have a better chance of getting to Palestine.

As discussed earlier, between 1933 and 1939 the National Socialist authorities encouraged Jewish citizens to emigrate even if they made it difficult on an individual level and robbed Jews of their assets. Zionist associations such as Mizrachi and its youth wing, Bnei Akiva, found ways to take advantage of this situation. In the 1930s, they established training centres in Germany to offer agricultural training for youngsters in preparation for emigration to kibbutzim in Palestine. Some of the young people who lived at Gwrych Castle initially came from Youth Aliyah training or holding centres in Germany.

The Hebrew term for these agricultural training centres is *hachshara* in the singular or *hachsharot* in the plural. Organisers such as Arieh Handler were looking for large farms or estates to house refugees and organise such activities, and found them in rural, often somewhat remote locations. A large *hachshara* accommodating nearly 200 young people was established at Whittingehame Farm in Scotland, on the estate of Lord Balfour. A similar number was housed at the Gwrych Castle *hachshara* in Abergele. Llandough Castle, near Cowbridge, was a smaller *hachshara* and eventually many of those who had settled there were resettled at Gwrych Castle. There were different Zionist groups organising and supporting training camps in the UK. Despite not allowing large-scale immigration into Palestine, the British government welcomed the training camps, especially after the start of the Second World War, as they provided young, able-bodied workers for agricultural work while young British men were joining the Armed Forces. This is another example of expediency meeting a humanitarian need and, as is often the case, it is difficult to decide whether the British authorities were more motivated by the fact that the Jewish teenagers were useful workers or by the fact that they needed to escape National Socialist persecution.

Most of the refugees housed at Llandough Castle had arrived on a Kindertransport. They were aged above twelve upon arrival and first housed at Great Engeham Farm in Kent, where they had to live in very basic barracks (vacated by the army) with earth floors and no heating or running hot water. Those that arrived later were accommodated in tents and disused railway carriages. Most refugees arrived at Great Engeham Farm during the summer months of 1939. However, when the autumn brought colder weather, conditions became desperate, and some of the young refugees started to suffer from ill health. A group of them was therefore transferred to Llandough Castle. The castle, which looked more like a large manor house than a medieval castle, was owned by the Byass family. In 1929, Lady Byass had let the castle to the Ministry of Labour, who used it for the recuperation of young Welsh men whose health had been damaged by working in the mines. At the outbreak of war, the Welsh youngsters were sent home to their families, and Lady Byass allowed refugees to be housed there instead. Llandough had an appealing exterior and conditions were pleasant, with electricity and heating and even a swimming pool, which had been built for physiotherapy purposes to aid the convalescence of the young miners. Most of the young refugees were very happy to leave the cold barracks and tents in Kent behind. At Llandough Castle, they received lessons, agricultural training and engaged in extra-curricular activities such as swimming and other sports.

Llandough is located in South Wales, not too far away from Cardiff, and its Jewish community. Members of this Jewish community were keen to offer hospitality to the young refugees and some were invited to spend the weekend with Jewish families in Cardiff. This sort of arrangement was not an uncommon occurrence all over the UK in view of the novelty of the recently arrived young refugees. It was a welcome distraction for some of the youngsters and helped them to practise their English language skills. However, because no one prepared the hosts nor the refugees as to what to expect from each other, there were some uncomfortable encounters as well.

There was often a general expectation on the behalf of members of the Anglo-Jewish community that the refugees had come from deprived and persecuted families. The refugees' families were certainly persecuted for being Jewish but the children and young people were not necessarily from deprived backgrounds. One young refugee noted her host family's surprise that she played the piano and knew Latin. In some cases, the young refugees felt that they were 'paraded' in front of dignitaries or members of the local Jewish communities and were used to show the hosts' generosity and commitment to do good. This particular group of young refugees were teenagers, and we can all imagine how uncomfortable this would feel at that age. Thus, the response to the hospitality that was extended by members of the nearby Jewish communities was a bit hit and miss. Some young refugees enjoyed it very much and relished the chance to practise English, to enjoy home comforts in a family setting and to establish contact with the Anglo-Jewish communities. Some host families clearly had more experiences with teenagers than others, taking them out to the cinema or for day trips which they generally enjoyed very much. Others, while most likely well-intentioned, expected impeccable behaviour from young people who had been removed from their familiar surroundings due to no fault of their own. Some were looking for an explicit demonstrative show of gratitude in response to their hospitality. In these cases, often both sides were disappointed.

Although the child refugees were happy enough with their accommodation at Llandough Castle, their stay came to an end after a relatively short period. This group of young refugees were moved out in 1940 when the building was requisitioned by the British government once more. The British authorities were looking for a place to house members of the Canadian Airforce near to the local airfield. Llandough Castle was an ideal place for this purpose due to its location and comfort. Its proximity to the military airfield would have been considered a drawback for its use as housing for anyone not in the Forces, as it was clearly in more danger of being bombed by the German air force than a house or hostel at a different location. Civilians were generally moved away from such areas if possible, and this might also have been a consideration in the decision to move the teenagers to Gwrych Castle. If the youngsters had been adult refugees many of them would have been considered enemy aliens and definitely moved away from the area, possibly to be interned on the Isle of Man. We do not know whether the fact that they were teenagers and on the cusp of being considered adults also played a part in moving most of them to the more sparsely populated and less militarily sensitive Abergele area.

The young refugees made the journey from Llandough Castle to Gwrych Castle by bus, and many noted the changing landscape on the journey north in their letters and diaries. Quite a few refugees also commented on the name of their new abode as well; Gwrych is more difficult to pronounce for a German or Czech speaker than Llandough. But not all of the new residents of Gwrych Castle came via Llandough Castle. Quite a few arrived straight from Great Engeham Farm in Kent, and a small number from other locations. Many of the teenage refugees, such as Erwin Seligmann, also commented on the imposing architecture of the castle:

> 'When our bus reached the main gate, an enormously high tower appeared in view, jutting out of the dark fog at night. We were reminded of one of those towers in the middle ages, where the unfortunate prisoners were kept starving.'

Gwrych Castle was built between 1812 and 1822 by Lloyd Hesketh Bamford-Hesketh. The castle passed then to the Dundonald family; however, by 1939, Lord Dundonald had not been using the property for over fifteen years and so he offered it for free to the Ministry of Labour and then to the British Forces. Both declined to take up the offer. However, as will be told in more detail below, permission was finally given on 28 August 1939 that the castle could be used to house refugee children. Unfortunately, as the castle had not been used for so long, it had fallen into disrepair. Moreover, it had probably never been kitted out with certain modern conveniences. Nevertheless, for those child refugees who arrived straight from the barracks and tents in Kent, the prospect of living in a castle initially must have seemed like a dream come true.

Walter Bingham, a Kindertransportee from Germany, later discussed his memories of being one of the first youngsters forming an advance party to Gwrych Castle from Great Engeham Farm. They were collected in red buses from the company Crossville, which operated services across the north-west of England and north to mid-Wales. When Walter first caught sight of Gwrych Castle he thought it was magnificent. He was particularly struck by the oak-panelled

159

entrance, a marble staircase, and rooms with very large open fireplaces. But reality set in very quickly: there was no electricity and totally inadequate toilet and bathroom facilities. The accommodation at Gwrych had been designed for an aristocratic family and handfuls of servants to support them, most likely less than 15 people. Now Gwrych Castle was expected to accommodate 200.

How had it come about that Gwrych Castle became a home for these children and teenagers? After the British civil and military authorities decided Gwrych was not suitable for their needs, it had been brought to the attention of Arieh Handler, a young Jewish man, born in 1915 in Brno in the present-day Czech Republic but working as an active Zionist organiser out of Germany. Handler had become active in the Zionist Youth movement in Germany in the early 1930s. He came from an Orthodox Jewish family but had attended mainly non-Jewish state schools in Magdeburg and Frankfurt as a boy and then a Yeshiva in Frankfurt, before studying at a Rabbinic Seminary in Berlin. Due to the persecution of the Jewish population in Germany after 1933, the Zionist movement there grew in strength and Handler was one of a number of activists who started to organise the training of young Jews for the agricultural sector to enable them to emigrate to Palestine.

What we sometimes struggle to acknowledge, with hindsight and our knowledge of the mass murder of the Holocaust, is the fact that the National Socialist regime did not immediately set out to murder all Jews after rising to power in 1933. The Nazi regime certainly aimed for a Germany that would be free of Jewish citizens but emigration was certainly one method that was being supported at the time. Young Zionists like Arieh Handler therefore travelled around Western Europe in order to try and find placements for young male and female German – and later Austrian and Czech – Jews on farms, or similar, to save them from persecution but also to train them for eventual emigration to Palestine. Handler stated in an interview many years later that he had permission from the German authorities to do this. He expressed surprise that he was trusted with such an important job but also that he, as a young Jewish man, was given the freedom to travel to countries such as the Netherlands, Sweden and Great Britain. Handler held strong views on the situation in Germany in the 1930s. He felt that if German Jewish leaders and German Jewish institutions had given greater support to his and other Zionist endeavours, he could have saved more Jewish youngsters. He argued that the term 'Kindertransport' is a belittling of the rescue operation he and others like him pursued and therefore he never took part in any post-war commemorative event despite living until 2011. For Handler, the most important consideration when finding ways to house and care for young refugees was preparing them to make Aliyah and build Eretz Israel. He was clear he did not want individual young refugees hosted by non-Jews, or in individual families, rather than living in communal settings, as this might take them away from the Jewish faith and the ongoing difficult task of building a Jewish state.

As we know, the Kindertransport was a quickly enacted visa waiver scheme which enabled the escape of over 10,000 underage refugees from Germany within ten months. While 80 per cent of the youngsters who came on the Kindertransport were Jewish, most of the foster placements on offer were with non-Jewish families. As described earlier, some of the sponsoring organisations asked the parents to sign a form that stated that they were happy for their Jewish child to be placed with non-Jewish foster families. These placements were criticised by many Orthodox organisers including Arieh Handler. He later described arguing with one of the prominent administrators at Bloomsbury House, the headquarters of many refugee organisations, who felt that the most important aim was simply to get as many children as possible away from National Socialist persecution and save their lives. Finding a placement that matched a child's religious affiliation was considered a secondary concern. Handler, on the other hand, felt that this was very important and that the young people should stay together and join *hachsharot* as, in his opinion, emigration to Palestine should be the ultimate aim. He argued that communal placements were preferable because it would prepare them for the communal life of the kibbutzim. Handler worried that living in a small family as a foster child would make them less suitable for the life that he envisaged for them in the new homeland in Palestine. Arieh Handler later argues this point in an interview:

'The main thing is to save lives. And if you have a non-Jewish family prepared to accept them, let's send them, wherever it is, they survive, and that's the most important thing, very logical. What was our argument? We said yes, if there is no other way, that is a way. But if we can find a way to place 200 boys and girls in a Castle which was then given to me for the duration of the war, Gwrych Castle, in North Wales, next to Abergele [...] If we can get such a place, and we can place 200 boys and girls there, in their surrounding, it is better than to put them to a family which has their own problems, because there is a war on. And I believe that we were right.'

The fact that many Kindertransportees did not remain 'in the Jewish fold' is something that some religious leaders regret of course, as did Arieh Handler. There are no official statistics, and the nature of religious observance is very difficult to define, but Handler's estimation that of the 10,000 child refugees who arrived only about 4,000 considered themselves religious Jews by the 1980s is possibly not far off. Certainly, about 20 per cent of those arrivals had come from families that did not define themselves as Jewish, but rather were externally and newly classified as such by Nazi race laws. Furthermore, the second half of the 20th century generally saw a move towards a more secular society and many Jews who had grown up in religious Anglo-Jewish families married non-Jewish partners and decided not to affiliate themselves either with Judaism as such or with religious observance. Therefore, if around 40 per cent of those who came to the UK on a Kindertransport remained religious

Jews, we might argue that this is approximately in line with general trends and not a reflection of the process by which they were placed with non-Jewish foster families. However, it needs to be remembered that we are only dealing with estimates; the information available is not sufficiently complete to make accurate statistical comparisons.

Having a preference for living in more communal settings might be seen as surprising, but it is one that many older child refugees expressed, regardless of whether they wanted to live in *hachsharot*. Study of the life stories and memoirs of the former child refugees does suggest that many of the older children and teenagers did prefer to live in communal settings, whether camps like Gwrych Castle or boarding schools and universities. They were often happy to get away from unfamiliar family rules and traditions and to live somewhere where they could give each other support and help each other adapt to their new lives.

Handler could only get larger numbers of refugee youngsters into the UK once the Kindertransport scheme was opened in December 1938. Before that, even if he could convince a farmer to take on a refugee trainee, he could not easily get such trainees a visa to come to the UK. Handler felt that, before the end of 1938, placing a teenage refugee as an agricultural trainee was much easier in Denmark or the Netherlands than in the UK. Once Britain was at war with Germany, the Kindertransport stopped, and it became difficult to travel at all. However, Handler did manage to bring in a small number of young refugees after September 1939 by getting them work permits for the UK. These were available because the British government realised that, as a consequence of so many able-bodied young people joining the army and auxiliary services, there was a labour shortage in the agricultural sector.

The *hachshara* at Gwrych Castle offered community to traumatised young people. Being part of a Zionist training camp also provided a sense of purpose, as did the involvement in practical work with the local community in Abergele. Handler felt that it was also important that the Jewish refugees were visible in the local area and useful to the local economy to gain acceptance and show their usefulness. In later life, Handler saw Gwrych as a successful venture and as an especially important *hachshara*, due to its size and the fact that accommodating the youngsters together kept them within a Jewish community and did not expose them to non-Jewish foster parents during the war.

Many who were initially accommodated there later rose to important positions and fulfilled important functions in Israel. Arieh Handler would later be present at the Declaration of Israel and became one of the 27 signatories, and some of the Gwrych youngsters would set up Kibbutz Lavi in Israel. Another former Gwrych Castle resident became the headteacher of an important education institution in Jerusalem.

The fact that the Gwrych Castle *hachshara* was closed unceremoniously in 1941 is given a different interpretation from different sides. Local historian Andrew Hesketh has suggested that most members were not sufficiently committed to the Zionist aim and preferred to leave the castle in Abergele, either to seek employment in more economically vibrant places such as Manchester or join relatives elsewhere in the UK. Certainly not all of them subsequently pursued emigration to Israel; many emigrated to the US and others stayed in the UK. Nevertheless, Hesketh also found that a number of former Gwrych residents had interesting careers and lives. Herman Rothman acted as an investigator at a trial of Nazi war criminals, Hanna Zuntz became an internationally acclaimed ceramicist and Walter Bingham played a wizard in the films *Harry Potter and the Philosopher's Stone* and *Harry Potter and the Chamber of Secrets*.

There were different routes from Germany into the *hachsharot* in Britain. Some youngsters joined a Kindertransport which eventually led to them being settled in a *hachshara* in the usual way, that is by their parents registering them with the local Jewish community and them being allocated a place. Others were selected after attending preparation camps organised by the Zionist movement, such as the preparation camp in Rüdnitz just outside Berlin or a Zionist camp in Hamburg-Blankenese, a suburb of Hamburg. Some of the youngsters describe a strict selection process, which resulted in them feeling privileged to be one of the chosen ones. These decisions were made by adults at the local level and were not always very easy to understand from the point of view of the young person. Some of the refugees later confirmed that Britain was really their second choice and that they had originally signed up for emigration to Palestine. They agreed to come to Britain only after the possibility of fulfilling their original goal was removed. Some even had visas to go to Palestine, which were cancelled by the British authorities.

Czech refugee Mimi Schleissner was 14 years old when she arrived first at Llandough. Shortly afterwards, she moved with the other children on to Gwrych Castle, where she was told that she would only need to stay in the UK for a short time before she would be able to emigrate to Palestine. She found this thought comforting as her parents were also trying to emigrate to Palestine, and she believed that they would all be reunited there in a matter of months.

Not all the young refugees stayed at Engeham Farm in Kent before travelling to Wales. They arrived at Liverpool Street station and were distributed to any accommodation that would be able to provide them with a bed for a few days. As the refugees destined for *hachsharot* were at least 12 or 13 years old, their care needs might have been considered less pressing than those of very young children. This meant that they sometimes ended up in completely unsuitable accommodation, such as a seamen's hostel, where they were left unsupervised and unprotected and had to mix with adults, who would drink alcohol to excess and use sexually explicit language.

Handler and other Youth Aliyah organisers were clearly very desperate to provide suitable accommodation; they sent an advance party to Gwrych Castle to prepare for the arrival of the teenage refugees even before they had had the official go-ahead that the castle could be used for such purposes. Arieh Handler's brother, Dr Julius Handler, who had studied medicine in both Germany and Switzerland, was part of the team of seven which included a British solicitor, David Smith, and others from the Zionist Youth movement, most of them refugees themselves. Smith had to act as an interpreter for other members of the group as their first language was not English, and some could barely speak it at all. None of the arrivals had any knowledge of Welsh. Having arrived at Gwrych Castle, Julius Handler described the situation as pretty desperate due to the lack of money or equipment. The castle had been left empty for a number of years and contained no furniture. It quickly became clear that each of the bedrooms would have to accommodate around six to eight youngsters if sufficient room for 200 was to be created. Although the dining room was large, it was not spacious enough to accommodate everyone in one sitting for meals. All these issues indicated that despite the castle's size, accommodating so many young people would be a challenge. The focus of the advance party was on sorting out the kitchen facilities and the water supply, which was described as 'erratic'.

Another member of the advance party was a young rabbi, Shmuel Sperber, who would soon be joined by his wife Miriam and their two very young children. The Gwrych *hachshara* therefore had the huge advantage of having its own rabbi making religious practice and religious instruction a lot easier than at other *hachsharot*. On 28 August 1939, Arieh Handler received confirmation that the castle could be used to house Kindertransport children. As soon as practically possible thereafter, the first young people arrived. And by 8 September 1939, the Gwrych *hachshara* had been fully established with 202 residents: 172 children and teenagers and 30 adults.

The first of the young refugees arrived at the castle on 31 August 1939. The new arrivals were astonished at its size and its grand medieval-style appearance, but also shocked at the building's condition and the lack of furniture, running water and toilets.

Several inhabitants describe their arrival at the castle in their memoirs, in which they reported that some of young refugees had to sleep on the bare floor during their first nights, and bathe in the sea in the morning. Osias Findling remembers:

> 'The castle hadn't been used for about 30 years. The dust was so high it went up to your ankles. We arrived about 5 o'clock in the morning. We slept on the bare floor but we had to move the dust to find a place to sleep.'

Pretty soon, however, local people helped out with furniture and blankets. A delivery arrived of items collected and donated by refugee committees, charities, and the Quakers. Then an order from Marks & Spencer with furniture included also arrived. After about two weeks, the older and stronger of the teenage refugees were ordered to help with the digging of field latrines. Of course, all of this was happening against the backdrop of the outbreak of the Second World War.

Many of the youngsters initially felt extremely lonely as they had been uprooted several times in short succession and most knew little about their fellow travellers. Although most of the refugees spoke German, there were some who only spoke Polish, and some from Czechoslovakia and even Latvia. Knowledge of Yiddish and Hebrew also varied. Some of the Youth Aliyah leaders did not necessarily see the process of uprooting the young people from a familiar life as a disadvantage; it would make it easier for them to become part of a Zionist community and learn to abide by different laws and rules. In order to encourage the self-sufficiency and maturity necessary for onward emigration to Palestine, the leaders felt that they had to establish structures, routines and a rapport quickly. They divided the youngsters in groups according to age: Group A for 16–17-year-olds, Group B for those aged approximately 14 to 15 and Group C for children aged under 14. The youngest resident at Gwrych was 12 years old.

All youngsters were supposed to attend lessons and religious instruction, and to carry out chores, such as cooking, cleaning and laundry. The school lessons were not always well organised since they were only a small number of adults to implement them. Later, they also had to work outside the castle, especially the older ones; chores were extremely monotonous, and the work as agricultural trainees was often very hard, even on the occasions when the weather was not inclement. Furthermore, all of the refugees were also worried about their family and friends left behind on the Continent. After a few months, some of the older teenagers were placed in proper apprenticeships with farmers, mechanics or the local hairdresser, which was no doubt useful for their future but added to their already heavy workload.

Nevertheless, the youngsters still found time to have fun. They explored and played in the castle's vast grounds, and the older and braver ones went to Abergele to find out about the local amenities. Initially, contact with the local population was not encouraged. In part, this was due to the fact that all the support staff and the teenagers had far too much lifetime experience of being persecuted because of their faith. In part, it was also because the *hachshara*'s Zionist stance would have demanded internal loyalty and distance from non-Jews.

There were certainly some locals who worried about the arrival of a large group of foreign youths, mostly German speaking, in September 1939. The war had just started and, as in many places in the UK, some people did not properly understand that Jewish refugees had been persecuted by the Nazis in the German Reich, and therefore were most unlikely to be supporters of, or spies for, the German enemy. Antisemitic prejudice was, of course, common in the UK as well as the rest of Europe at the time so, for some locals, the fact that the youths were Jewish was worrying. The number of Jews living in the towns on the North Wales coast such as Rhyl, Bangor and Llandudno was not insignificant and had an established history. Llandudno attracted many Jewish visitors on holiday and had a synagogue, a number of Jewish-owned shops and at least one kosher hotel at the time. During the war years, the resort was popular with Jewish families who were keen to escape the bombings in London and Liverpool, which meant that the number of Jewish residents increased markedly. Apparently, it was even known colloquially as 'Little Jerusalem'. One of the established businesses was the Wartski chain of jewellery, art and fashion shops in Bangor and Llandudno. Isidore Wartski was a long-standing member of Bangor Town Council and became mayor of Bangor in 1939. So, the story of the Jews and acceptance of them in North Wales is clearly a complicated one. Former Plaid Cymru Deputy Vice President, William John Gruffydd, wrote a hostile editorial in Welsh language paper *Y Llenor*:

'North Wales is full of wealthy, scheming Jews who arrogate to themselves all the resources of the land, leaving the native population helpless and impoverished... And by the way, is it not high time that somebody protested loudly against those Jews who oppress Llandudno, Colwyn Bay, Abergele and the surrounding countryside?'

It seems, however, that the local population of Abergele did not feel the same way and proved to be a friendly bunch. They were sympathetic and curious regarding the new residents of Gwrych Castle. The local policeman was horrified when some of the refugees ran away from him when he approached them for a chat in Abergele, presumably because they had had traumatic experiences with Nazi authority figures in uniform. He decided to visit the castle with cake and explain the role of a community policeman to the residents. Shopkeepers and passers-by would speak to the young refugees in Welsh and English and would occasionally give them small treats. The local use of the Welsh language is remarked on in several memoirs of the time their authors spent at the castle. Most of the refugees did not realise before they arrived in Abergele that

Wales had its own language. When they initially could not understand what some locals were saying they thought that this was due to the fact that they had been taught English badly, and not because the locals were speaking a completely different language. However, many of the teenage refugees were already at least bilingual and learning additional languages was nothing new to them, so they learnt some Welsh. We do not know what stage of fluency they reached, but it is reported that some of the young refugees won prizes at the local eisteddfod. Some later explained that they felt that they were given extra treats if they interacted with the farmers in Welsh. Henry Glanz remembered: '[we] found that we got away with murder if you spoke to them in Welsh, so we learnt as much Welsh as we could.'

Another attraction in Abergele was the cinema, which the teenagers were allowed to attend in small groups and as a special treat, having been given money for tickets from the *hachshara* funds. The cinema owner was very friendly and sometimes let them watch films for free if there were empty seats. One of the older boys was given the job of rewinding the reel in return for free admission by the cinema owner. Other slightly more irregular activities also took place. Although Abergele is not very far from Gwrych Castle on foot, some mischievous youngsters tried to stow away in delivery vans and other vehicles whenever they could to get lifts to town. Looking back on his time at Gwrych from the 1980s, one former refugee resident, John Edelnand, was exuberant in his praise for the local Welsh people. He felt that the locals were hospitable and kind and treated the young refugees as fellow human beings which, he emphasised, they needed badly after the traumatic experiences they had had in their home countries. Edelnand believed that a genuine bond had been created between the youngsters and Abergele. He was certainly not the only former refugee who maintained his relationship with the locality and some of the local residents. Quite a number of the former residents visited the castle after the war.

Inside the castle and the grounds, playing games such as hide and seek and a variety of sports were further popular activities. Indoors, the residents found a large wooden contraption that was repurposed as a table tennis table. Inter-group and inter-room tournaments followed. Football was a very popular sport and a Castle First XI team was established. It was made up primarily of teenage refugees and a few of the younger support workers. By December 1939, they had played their fourth game against local teams outside the castle and they had won all four.

Besides Jewish festivals and a Shabbat routine, the castle's leaders established modern traditions such as dance and music nights on Saturday evenings. Julius Handler was a passionate musician and a few youngsters had brought instruments with them. The local community kindly donated further instruments and an orchestra was formed. They practised, and apparently got quite good over time.

A lot of what we know about the Gwrych Castle *hachshara* comes from memoirs and oral history interviews, there are few contemporary documents. One exception is the castle newsletter founded by three young refugees, Erich Roper, Willy Braun and Bernhard Liwerant, and first published in October 1939. Entitled *Da'at ha-evrah* and written in Hebrew, German and English, the newsletter contained notices from the castle leaders, some articles with a Zionist message, reports about recent events, and many random pieces clearly submitted by anyone who fancied contributing. From this newsletter, we know that a big Zionist gathering of representatives from nine different *hachsharot* at Gwrych Castle, a so-called *pegisha*, took place. This was both a celebration of the movement and a forum to discuss challenges and make joint plans for the future. It was a great honour for the newest *hachshara* to be allowed to host this meeting. At the same time, it was not entirely surprising as Arieh Handler was one of the major national organisers of the Zionist movement, and he was obviously closely linked with Gwrych Castle. The *pegisha* was deemed to have been a great success.

The start of 1940 saw food shortages, especially shortages of butter and sugar, and the introduction of ration books. The memoirs and surviving letters from the refugees' time at the castle include frequent complaints about the food. As it was the teenagers themselves doing the cooking, aided and abetted by supervisors were also all very young and inexperienced, it is hardly surprising that the output was variable. There were also many complaints about the freezing conditions. January 1940 was one of the coldest months on record in the UK; the River Thames froze over in London. Life in the castle, with its inadequate insulation and heating system, must have been hard during the course of that bitter winter.

As we have seen, the locals were generally very friendly towards the castle residents and were aware of their difficult position living away from their families. People from Abergele donated second-hand items, and organisations such as the Llandudno Women's Zionist & Welfare Society collected clothing and money for them. The money was very welcome for the upkeep of the community but those who meant well by donating their cast-off clothes might have not quite understood the realities of life at the castle, the age of the residents or the manual work they were engaged in. One such donation is said to have consisted mainly of formal ladies' dresses and gentleman's suits which caused much hilarity among the teenagers but did not really help to keep them warm. However, this donation did come in handy for dressing up games. During the Purim Festival on 23 March 1940, they had the customary costume party and games, and there are some photos of laughing castle residents in exotic attire.

Photos survive from other festivities as well. The end of April 1940 brought the important Pesach celebration. During Pesach, Jews commemorate their escape from Egyptian servitude some 3,000 year ago, as told in the Book of Exodus in the Hebrew Scriptures. Observant Jews avoid leavened bread during the festival and instead bake the *matzah*, a thin, cracker-like unleavened bread.

Because the castle's cooking facilities were not up to this particular task, the baking was moved to the yard of the castle. There is a photo that shows Rabbi Sperber with a large crowd of children and the rudimentary oven on 23 April, probably in the process of passing the Hamotzi blessing. We can only imagine how the youngsters must have felt during such a celebration, which they would previously have celebrated with their families.

The experience of community with many other people of a similar age, who had had to cope with similar situations in their home countries, was one benefit of living at Gwrych Castle. There were, however, several downsides to having mainly other teenagers as your frame of reference. There was clearly a lack of supervision at times, and that might have led to experiences of bullying that remained unchecked. There are also reports that some of the teenagers formed ill-advised sexual relationships with each other, possibly resulting in at least one pregnancy. Probably the most tragic occurrence at the castle was the death of David Kowalski, who was only twelve years old. He had fled from the German town of Halberstadt with two others and is said to have been the youngest resident of the Gwrych *hachshara*. When he fell seriously ill, he was moved to a hospital in Liverpool, but sadly he did not recover and he died. The castle newsletter carried an obituary, which describes him as serious-minded and the cause of his death an insidious disease.

One of the former Gwrych residents, Ruth Wesson, has more negative memories of her time in North Wales than many others. Later, she recalled that many of the teenagers fell ill and she blamed this on the difficult sanitary and heating situation in the castle, the inadequate food and the lack of adult supervision. She felt that schooling was virtually non-existent and that the adults who were supposed to supervise the teenagers were largely occupied with their own affairs. Little is known about the precise cause of David's death and whether any of the adverse circumstances mentioned by Ruth had any bearing on this tragic loss of life. However, David's death shows that Gwrych *hachshara* had its tragedies as well as its positive sides. Ruth Wesson's negative memories provide balance to our understanding of the Gwrych Castle experience. This is very important because there is a tendency among commentators and historians to overemphasise the positive aspects of the Kindertransport operation and to gloss over the difficulties and its tragic consequences for some of the children.

Another less than glorious episode in British wartime history is the story of the internment of enemy aliens. Closely following the outbreak of the Second World War, the Aliens Department of the Home Office implemented a policy of establishing tribunals which would decide whether non-British citizens posed a threat to the state during wartime. There were three categories in which the tribunal was required to place the individual: Category A for people who were a serious danger and should be interned immediately; an intermediate Category B which meant individuals were not interned but restrictions such as a travel ban would be imposed on them; and Category C for those who were not deemed to pose a threat at all, and therefore were neither placed under restrictions nor in internment camps. Gwrych Castle residents over the age of 16, regardless of whether they were male or female, refugee or staff, had to travel to Caernarfon and appear in front of the local tribunal when asked to do so. Most were put in Category C, but a sizeable number, even though they were known refugees from National Socialism, were placed in Category B.

While most of the Category B restrictions that were placed on the Gwrych residents in late 1939 and early 1940 were not too severe, the situation changed as the war developed. There was pressure from the public and some media outlets, such as the *Liverpool Daily Post*, which speculated that a so-called Fifth column was active in North Wales in January 1940. After the Battle of Dunkirk, the government responded by changing its policy and deciding that all enemy aliens should be interned.

On 21 June 1940, the Chief Constable of Colwyn Bay, accompanied by several policemen, arrived at Gwrych Castle and took away a number of residents. They were marched through Abergele and then transported to Liverpool. This was repeated several times until 26 June 1940. Some of those interned ended up in the Hutchinson Camp on the Isle of Man, while some 'volunteered' to be transported abroad. Several *hachshara* residents ended up on the *HMT Dunera* destined for Australia. This particular voyage has subsequently become notorious for its terrible conditions and the mistreatment of the internees. After their arrival in Australia they were imprisoned in Hay Camp in New South Wales.

During these raids on the castle, the Chief Constable did not arrest any of the support workers, as he recognised that they were needed to look after the sizeable group of underage refugees at the castle. The last residents taken away for internment were extremely unlucky as the British government was in the process of revoking the policy of universal internment by June 1941. Julius Handler described the awful experience of having to say goodbye to the same youngsters they had managed to save from imprisonment in their native countries. The fear the refugees themselves must have felt is difficult to imagine. Having escaped Nazi-dominated Central Europe, they were now being arrested and faced an unknown fate at the hand of the British authorities; it must have been extremely traumatic. It was also detrimental to the sense of community and purpose of the Gwrych Castle *hachshara*.

Not entirely surprisingly, less is known about the end of the Gwrych Castle *hachshara* than about the beginning. We know that by September 1941 it had closed its doors and the last child refugee and adult supervisor had left. The fact that many of those who had turned 18 had been interned and that some now lived thousands of miles away was the determining reason for the steady decline in numbers. Since the arrival of the refugees from Llandough Castle, there had only been very occasional arrivals from other *hachsharot*.

No new refugees were arriving – it was almost impossible to reach the UK as a refugee during wartime – and the chances of making Aliyah to Palestine were also extremely slim. Most of Europe was occupied by Nazi Germany, an extremely depressing situation for all Gwrych residents. Departures of those turning 18 happened due to internment but also because individuals wanted to take their fate into their own hands. Some wanted to join friends or family members who lived elsewhere in the UK, while others wanted to get more satisfying and better paid employment. The Gwrych leadership had made the decision that the youngsters would work for free for the local farmers and local businesses. There were several reasons for this. In the first place, the teenagers had little experience or training and could only fulfil the most basic duties and so there was little basis on which to claim pay. Also, by making no charge, placements could easily be found for all of them as there were always businesses or farms prepared to accept free labour. After a while, some of the youngsters got very proficient but the leadership still opposed allowing them to be paid. Some of the employers secretly paid their workers in kind, but it is obvious that some of those who turned 18 during this time felt that they wanted – and deserved – to earn a proper wage. Others might also have lost faith in the Zionist project. With no end of the hostilities in sight, and no way of knowing if or when they would be allowed to emigrate to Palestine, some probably changed their plans and decided to build their lives in the UK. From what evidence there is, it is apparent that the leadership was committed to Zionism and preparing for Aliyah, but there is no way of knowing how many of the young refugees were equally committed to the idea, or indeed if any had simply agreed to be part of a *hachshara* as a means of escaping Nazi-dominated Europe, something they all desperately needed to do.

According to Ruth Wesson's memories, the living conditions at the castle did not improve much over the years. Yes, there were toilets and a stove, and the castle owner contributed to roof repairs, but the building remained difficult to heat and some of the accommodation remained basic. It is reasonable to speculate that some youngsters probably preferred to find themselves more comfortable housing, which would be open to them if they managed to earn a reasonable wage. The *hachshara* leadership never had enough money to really improve the living quarters at the castle. On top of this, David Smith, the only English member of the castle leadership team tragically died at that time in a car accident. This left a gaping hole in the supervisory team as he had been good at finding funding from outside the Zionist movement.

Gwrych Castle also turned out to be extremely expensive to run. What had attracted Arieh Handler to the premises – its spaciousness and remote location – meant it had higher running costs than some smaller *hachsharot*. Therefore, the national leadership seems to have decided that the remaining Gwrych residents were to be moved to other training centres. Dr Julius Handler also left and took up a position at a hospital in Wrexham. No single event marked the final closure of the Gwrych *hachshara*; however, the community gradually dispersed between March and September 1941. In fact, this episode in local history was largely forgotten until well into the 21st century.

On occasion, former refugees have visited Gwrych Castle and Abergele, and a number of them have published memoirs or given interviews discussing it. The castle itself went through a number of uses in the second half of the 20th century but was never comprehensively restored. Dr Mark Baker, an architectural historian, founded the Gwrych Preservation Trust in 1997 to work on the restoration of the Gwrych Castle, which has been ongoing ever since. The castle is not as well known a historic monument as we might expect. It only received its first mention on a brown road sign indicating the presence of historic monument or tourist attraction in October 2021. This was a year after Gwrych Castle had come to the attention of the national UK media when the television channel ITV announced that its popular television series *I'm a Celebrity Get Me Out of Here* was to be set there rather than in Australia as it had been in previous years. This was a consequence of travel restrictions related to the COVID 19 pandemic. Gwrych Castle remained the location for the show in 2021. Some newspaper articles about the programme mentioned that Gwrych had accommodated young Jewish refugees and one even featured an interview with the then 90-year-old Harry Glanz, who had been one of the youngsters who ran away from the local policeman while living at the castle. At the time of the interview, Glanz was living near Worthing in England, one of the last surviving residents of the Gwrych Castle *hachshara*. He talked about watching the show on TV:

'I watched it last night to see what parts of the castle I recognised. It feels strange to see them in the castle that was my safe haven. For them it's a game. For me, it was a life-changing refuge.'

Internment of Civilians in Britain during the Second World War
(© IWM HU36122) – Internees returning to their camp on the seafront
in Douglas, Isle of Man. Military officials check their numbers
as they pass through the barricade

Memorial to the Kindertransport at Liverpool St Station, 2022
(© Morris Brodie)

'WHAT IS SWANSEA?': THE STORY OF KÄRRY WERTHEIM – WHO BECAME ELLEN DAVIS

The majority of refugees from National Socialism who came to Wales were Jewish, but most were not from Orthodox backgrounds. This was true for most of the child refugees who fled to the UK via the Kindertransport scheme. The selection of suitable candidates for a Kindertransport was made by the German and Austrian Jewish communities in the case of Jewish children, or the local Quaker or Christian partners in the case of those families who were persecuted as Jewish but did not define themselves as Jewish. It was less likely that a child from an Orthodox family would escape in this way. It seems that Orthodox parents were possibly not so open to the idea of letting their children flee as unaccompanied minors, given the significant role family plays in Orthodox Judaism. Additionally, the Kindertransport organisers in the UK, the Refugee Children's Movement (RCM), were not able to guarantee foster placements in Orthodox families. They were unable even to guarantee foster placements in Jewish families. The vast majority of foster families who volunteered to take care of a child refugee were not Jewish. The Continental organisers actually asked the birth parents to sign a permission form to enable their children to be fostered by Christian families (see earlier). This made the process very difficult for many Orthodox families who wanted their children to grow up within the faith. Some Orthodox Jewish children managed to flee on a Kindertransport as part of an Orthodox group – such as the ones organised by Rabbi Solomon Schönfeld, who managed to organise communal placements where they stayed together after their arrival in the UK. Some Orthodox children did end up with Orthodox foster parents, but this was often more by luck than by design, as was the case for Kärry Wertheim, who was born in 1929 into an Orthodox Jewish family in Germany. Kärry's foster mother changed her name after her arrival in the UK and she became Ellen; a name which she kept. To make things less confusing, I will use the name Ellen throughout the story.

Ellen grew up in a large Orthodox Jewish family as the oldest of six siblings. Her early childhood was in many ways idyllic. She lived in a large house and garden in a rural location with her mother Johanna and her father Julius, her maternal grandparents, whose surname was Kaiser, and one aunt and five uncles. Their home was in Hoof, a small village located on the main route to the city of Kassel in the state of Hesse in Western Germany. They lived in a building that was made up of two houses, to accommodate the whole family, and Ellen remembers playing in a small stream in the garden of their home. Her grandfather was a Jewish butcher, a *shochett*, someone who slaughters animals according to Jewish religious law. Together with his sons, he either sold the meat in the small shop attached to their house or travelled to the city of Kassel to sell it at market. Ellen remembers her grandmother as a large kind woman with white hair and a white pinafore who organised the house, comforted the children when they hurt themselves at play, cooked, baked, and lit the Shabbat meal candles every Saturday.

While the Jewish population in Austria was largely concentrated in the cities, and especially in Vienna, there were many rural Jewish communities in Germany. Even small villages like Hoof had a Jewish grocery store, remembered by Ellen for its enticing smell, and a synagogue, which she thought was beautiful.

They lived the traditional life of a religious Jewish family, a life in which the men dominated the lives of the women. Ellen was the first child of her young mother and father, and another sibling was born every year after her birth, despite the fact that her mother suffered from debilitating varicose veins while pregnant. Ellen took on the role of a young carer; as the eldest daughter, she looked after her siblings as soon as they were born and also looked after her mother when she was ill during her pregnancies. Ellen never had a toy doll, instead she played with her baby brothers and sister. Ellen felt a great deal of love for her younger siblings, she felt responsible for their welfare and they had a relationship different from the average sibling relationship.

Ellen's grandfather was the head of the extended family and made decisions on all matters in public and in the home; he expected obedience from all members of the family. Ellen's father Julius was clearly an independent and somewhat rogue element within the family. He had mainly non-Jewish friends and he only joined his in-laws and his wife in the synagogue on high holidays. He did not work for the family business. Instead he was keen on sport, boxing and bodybuilding and spent a lot of time outside the home. Ellen's mother Johanna clearly accepted this behaviour and admired her husband despite his lack of commitment and willingness to take responsibility for his family, which he did neither in practical nor in financial terms. He did not help care for the children nor did he carry out household tasks. It seems Julius saw the beginning and end of his duties as consisting of getting Johanna pregnant. There was one exception; when he was present in the home, Julius oversaw the disciplining of his children. Not unusually for the time, this meant corporal punishment with a belt.

Before 1933, the family was well-liked in the village and interacted with their non-Jewish neighbours in a cooperative and friendly manner, joining in with communal activities. All the villagers brought their bread dough to the communal bakehouse attached to a bakery shop where their loaves would be baked together in a large oven. Ellen's grandmother joined in this activity, which also was a good opportunity to talk with the other women. Her grandmother also brought the plaited bread dough for the Sabbath ritual to the bakehouse, picking it up when it was baked. Their religious practice was open for all to see and was accepted in the community. A neighbour in the village acted as Sabbath maid to the family. This meant she carried out activities that Jewish law forbade the family to carry out such as switching the lights on and off and clearing away after the meal and washing up.

Many of the accounts of Jewish children and young people who grew up in Germany in the first half of the 1930s describe a sudden change in their relationships with other children and neighbours after the National Socialists took power in January 1933. At first glance, this seems surprising: the history of anti-Semitism in Central Europe is long and it is difficult to comprehend that they changed their minds about their neighbours overnight. However, for a young child the change might well have appeared to be very sudden. If they hadn't grown up in a family that discussed politics and followed the news on the radio or in newspapers, the political development must have seemed rapid and surprising. This is what happened to Ellen: the village children were her friends and she was playing with them as usual. She remembers that suddenly some of them shouted swear words at her and excluded her from their games. Some of them called her 'dirty Jew' and physically attacked her. Before she even understood what a Nazi was, she and her family suffered serious harassment and exclusion. Ellen overheard the local policeman talking to her father Julius. He had come to their home to explain how her father should no longer speak to him in a familiar way, despite them having been friends for years; he added that Julius should also prevent his children from calling him 'uncle'. Pressure was clearly mounting on those who had Jewish friends to stop associating with them. Ellen's father encouraged her to fight back when attacked by other children and tried to teach her to box to defend herself and her siblings. Julius himself was arrested and spent time in camps including Dachau. He was released after a few weeks and then re-arrested.

When Ellen was five, she began to attend the two-room village school. As is customary in Germany, she received a large cardboard cone filled with sweets on her first day. Like many children, Ellen was excited to experience this rite of passage. By 1934, the Nazi flag with the swastika had been raised in the schoolyard and the non-

Jewish children and the teachers would no longer interact with the Jewish minority in Hoof. Instead, the Jewish children were forced to sit at the back of the class and made to stay in the classroom during breaktime rather than joining the others in the schoolyard. Her younger brother joined Ellen for a few months during the next academic year, but they stopped going to school altogether after the passing of the Nuremberg Laws in 1935.

As well as public pressure, another consequence of these new restrictions on Jewish citizens was that Jewish businesses were forced to close. Ellen's grandfather's butchery business ceased trading which led to him to look for ways to leave Germany. He could no longer see a future for himself in Germany, despite the fact that his family had lived in the village of Hoof since 1760 and that he had fought for Germany in the First World War.

As discussed elsewhere in this book, it was extremely difficult to obtain the necessary entry visa and work permit for any country in Europe and further afield. Most countries were afraid to admit large numbers of Jewish refugees and put high hurdles in their way. While the National Socialist dictatorship encouraged Jewish emigration at that time, it also demanded the completion of lengthy paperwork before emigration was permitted and tried to financially exploit the desperate Jewish Germans by demanding that all their usual taxes were paid before giving them permission to leave. The German government even charged a Reichsfluchtsteuer, a 'flight' tax. The final problem for those trying to flee was obtaining tickets for travel, especially if the destination was far afield. Ellen's Kaiser grandparents managed to obtain a visa for emigration to Argentina. They then had to immediately pay for the passage because there were not many places left on one of the passenger ships. This they did, and therefore they left quickly. It was the intention of the grandparents to send for the rest of the family when they could afford it and when they had obtained further visas. But unfortunately, as was the case with most Jewish refugees in this position, the situation in the host country Argentina did not make obtaining further funds or visas easy. From autumn 1939 onwards, the outbreak of the Second World War made further emigration virtually impossible.

The departure of the grandparents clearly had a negative effect on the rest of the family. The specific structure of the Kaiser family meant the grandfather's business had provided most of the income for the extended family and employment opportunities for his sons, while the matriarch had overseen organising the household and provided a lot of the emotional labour. Without them, and surrounded by a now largely hostile village community, things quickly deteriorated for all, but the situation of the youngest, of Ellen and her siblings, became especially difficult. Ellen's mother was ill, and her father largely absent, and there was no money coming in.

As described in other refugee stories in this book, the November Pogrom in 1938 was a watershed moment for Ellen's and many Jewish families. The experience of finding themselves completely unprotected against violent attack forced many to decide to part from their children in order for them to be able to leave Germany and find safety in the UK. In the case of Hoof, this turning point had been reached as early as December 1937 when a group of Hitler Youth violently attacked the synagogue in the village. After that incident, Ellen, her sister Ruth, and her brothers Rolf, Heinz, and Sally were sent to the Jewish Orphanage in Kassel in the hope that they would find support and safety there. The baby, Ludwig, stayed with his mother in Hoof.

Unfortunately, the move to Kassel did not protect the children from violent attack. As in many other towns, the widely known location of Jewish orphanages acted as a magnet for those intending to perpetrate violence against Jews. This meant the children and their adult carers were always fearful of attacks and only rarely ventured out. In the orphanage, Ellen continued in her role as oldest child, carer, and protector of her siblings. The Nazi State clearly wasn't going to support Jewish orphanages with funds or provisions, and Jewish charitable organisations hardly had the capacity to help at this point. By 1938, it was illegal for Jews to buy food in non-Jewish shops. Seeing how everyone in the orphanage was hungry, Ellen, then aged nine, and her brother Rolf, aged eight, volunteered to go shopping on behalf of them all. They managed to do this for two months without incident. Eventually, however, they were attacked by a group of Hitler Youth and beaten up. Ellen suffered kidney damage that had a detrimental effect on her for the rest of her life.

After this incident, and an arson attack during the November Pogrom on 9 November 1938, it is not surprising that the orphanage supervisor arranged for the Wertheim children to be considered for a Kindertransport to the UK. All the Wertheim children's photographs were taken for selection purposes, but it was Ellen who was eventually chosen. Her father started to visit the orphanage, appearing one day out of the blue, in an emaciated state and with a shaven head. Ellen remembers how he took her to various offices for papers to be signed, which must have been her application for a place on a Kindertransport. Ellen was not given any explanation as to the plans for her future. She was able to say a brief goodbye to both her parents and her youngest brother Ludwig before being driven to a train station to start her journey to the UK.

It is very difficult to imagine how bewildering this experience must have been for Ellen. She had never been on a train before; in fact, she had never even seen a train before. She had spent the first ten years of her life in circumstances that prevented her from venturing far from her family, her village, and later the orphanage. She had never seen the sea, did not know how ships or ferries worked, and had certainly never left Germany. When she tried to remember the journey years later, Ellen stated that she had very little recollection of the detail and recounted an anecdote explaining that she had tried to eat a banana without peeling it because she had never seen such a fruit before. This complete bewilderment continued when she was picked up in London by her foster father who took her on yet another train. This time it was a train to Swansea. She did not understand any English, of course. She remembers in her memoir that she had no idea about her destination: 'WHAT WAS SWANSEA? As we entered the train in London, I heard a man, as he wandered up and down outside, shouting Swansea, Swansea. I had no idea what he was saying, but I was struck by the word and the funny voice he had. When our long journey ended, there was another man shouting Swansea. He sounded very different. So again, what was Swansea?' Well, Swansea was the town that would become her home for the rest of her life.

Ellen was fostered by a childless Jewish couple. Her foster father had emigrated from Russia earlier in the 20th century and he had a business making accessories for ladies' clothes. Ellen remembered that he was devoted to studying and his books. Her foster mother liked going to the cinema and playing bridge. Ellen liked her foster father, who she described as gentle and kind, but did not get on so well with her foster mother, whom she described as stiff, distant and uncaring. The housework was largely left to their maid Phyllis. In her early days in Swansea, Ellen constantly thought of her siblings left behind in Germany. In her memories, she always refers to them as her 'children'. She had clearly seen herself in a mother-like caring role in regard to her brothers and sisters. For example, when she was first led into the dining room to find a table laden with food, Ellen immediately thought of 'her children' and how much they would enjoy such food, which seemed enough to feed the whole orphanage in Kassel.

Ellen suffered a huge culture shock and found it difficult to adapt to her new situation. Even though her foster parents were Jewish, there were many differences that led to challenges and misunderstandings. Her foster mother was clearly very unprepared for the experience as well and felt it necessary straight away to try and impose her ideas on the child. She cut off Ellen's plaits and, as mentioned at the start of this narrative, immediately changed her name to Ellen. Ellen did not speak any English and felt that whatever she did she could not please her foster mother. Ellen eventually made friends with the maid Phyllis, who was more physically affectionate and would hug and kiss her, which she found comforting. Ellen also got on well with some of the young workers who sewed buttons onto dresses in a workshop attached to the house.

On Saturday morning, the family went to the synagogue in Swansea, and on Sunday morning, Ellen went to a *cheder*, where Jewish children received religious instruction and learnt Hebrew. Ellen remembers that she was more advanced in Hebrew than the children in Swansea. Hearing the prayers in Hebrew was a comfort to her as it reminded her of her birth family and her home village, where attending synagogue had been such an important part of her life. Her foster father did not approve of the methods of the *cheder* teacher, who frequently hit the students on the knuckles, and eventually started taking her for walks on the beach every Sunday morning instead of sending her to the lessons.

In August 1939, Ellen received a postcard from her mother announcing that Ellen now had a new baby sister called Zilla. After that there were no more communications, as sending and receiving mail to and from the Continent was very difficult after the outbreak of war. However, Ellen also received a postcard from her father from the Isle of Man during the summer of 1939. Julius had managed to escape Germany and was now interned as an enemy alien on the Isle of Man. He even managed to visit her in Swansea several times and, despite him being a somewhat remote parent, she was very happy about these visits. Eventually, however, Julius was sent to Australia on the *HMT Dunera*, on a voyage that has become notorious for its bad conditions and ill treatment of internees. Ellen did not hear again from him for some years. After a lengthy silence concerning the fate of her mother and her siblings, Ellen received a letter from the Red Cross just after her 13th birthday. She learnt that her mother Johanna, her brothers Rolf, Heinz, Sally and Ludwig, and her sisters Ruth and Zilla, had been deported on one of the first transports to

Riga and subsequently murdered in a concentration camp. Ellen was absolutely devastated by the news and remembers that she read the letter a thousand times. A few weeks later, the house in Swansea was bombed and the Red Cross letter was lost, which actually came as something of a relief to Ellen since she couldn't look at it anymore. She was glad, however, that she managed to save the only photograph she had of herself with her mother and her siblings in Hoof.

Despite the fact that Ellen was placed with a family that was Jewish, which might have been expected to help her adapt to life in the UK, Ellen's childhood was marred by difficulty. Even when she met two other refugee children, a girl named Erika from Austria and a boy named Henry, she did not manage to establish friendships as their families were from different class backgrounds and they looked down on her as inferior. This clearly shows that while religious convictions and adherence to Jewish faith and culture were factors that might help a child to integrate into a new environment, they were by no means the only considerations. After being bombed out, the family had to move several times during the war years: first, to the Mumbles, and then to Sketty. In some areas of Swansea, Ellen found it easier to make friends than in others. Eventually, she joined a Jewish Youth Club, which was a very positive experience for her. She was elected a representative on the Swansea Youth Council. There she met her best friend Jean and started a friendship which lasted into old age.

After school, Ellen studied typing and shorthand at Clark's Commercial College and, after passing her exams, she got her first job, which gave her an income and independence from her foster mother. Ellen's foster father had died during the Second World War; however, her relationship with her mother did not get any better and she tried everything she could to be able to leave home. Ellen remembers feeling suicidal at one time and believes she would not have managed without her friend Jean.

As for many young women at that time, escape from the family home came via marriage. The son of her foster mother's sister, a young man called Sid, proposed to Ellen. With hindsight, longing to escape from her controlling foster mother was most likely not the best reason to agree to a proposal of marriage – their marriage was not a happy one. Ellen had continued to correspond with her biological father while he was incarcerated in an internment camp in the Australian desert and she managed to get his permission to marry. Julius sent her a small cheque and informed her that he had just re-married himself. Ellen and Sid were wed on 27 May 1948 in the Masonic Hall in Swansea. The couple spent their wedding night in the Mermaid Hotel on the Mumbles and their honeymoon in a Jewish hotel in Bournemouth. Neither Sid nor Ellen had any knowledge of sexual relationships and this side of the union proved a disaster and made Ellen very unhappy. After they returned to Swansea, they found a house and a few months later Ellen found out that she was pregnant. However, it turned out that Sid did not want children and so she kept the pregnancy hidden from him for some time. Ellen experienced an overwhelming feeling of love for her newborn daughter Anita. She worked from home, repairing stockings with a knitting machine, trying to earn money while also being responsible for the housework and childcare. Sid remained unenthusiastic about fatherhood; he seemed, in fact, a replica of Ellen's birth father Julius, being equally uninterested in his child or providing for his family. Nevertheless, Ellen wanted a second child and went on to have a boy called Martin. Throughout the pregnancy, she suffered with kidney problems as a consequence of the occasion when she had been beaten up by members of the Hitler Youth as a child in Germany.

Neither her physical ailments nor her unhappy marriage held Ellen back, however. She invested her savings of £50 in opening a shop in St Helen's Road in Swansea and started selling knitting machines. She travelled to London to meet the knitting machine manufacturers and became gradually more confident in herself. Unfortunately, she made a mistake when setting up the business by putting it in both her and Sid's names, which gave him access to her accounts. Two years later, when she wanted to use some of the money earned to visit her relatives in Argentina, it became apparent that Sid had emptied out the company's coffers. Although she had to give up the shop because of health problems, it is clear that succeeding at work had provided Ellen with the confidence and satisfaction that was missing from her role as a wife. Ellen always found it easy to find new jobs and enjoyed most of them. Despite being a working mother, Ellen had a good relationship with her children, but eventually, in 1968, she separated from Sid. Initially, after the break-up, Martin lived with Sid, which was very difficult for Ellen, but after a few months he came to live with his mother. Sid refused to divorce her, but Ellen found a new partner in Colin, who was also separated.

In later life, Ellen travelled extensively and reconnected with relatives in South America and the US. She also travelled to Israel and to Germany. Ellen found her visit to Germany very stressful. She was presented with a copy of the Red Cross letter informing her of the death of her mother and siblings, and she felt very ill at ease. After this one visit, she decided that she never wanted to visit Germany again. It did not mean, though, that she was not interested in educating others about the Holocaust. In 1997, an exhibition about Anne Frank was shown in Swansea. Ellen was approached by the Local Education Authority and asked whether she would give talks to school groups who visited the exhibition. This she agreed to and she found the experience very rewarding, and therefore she continued in her role as an educator:

'By 2003, I had lectured to almost seven thousand children. I accept no money for what I do [...] My love of children has never wavered. Still I must tell them of the horrors of my past life. It is the only way I can make them understand the importance of what to avoid in the future.'

Ellen had felt a sense of guilt ever since she had arrived in Swansea. This phenomenon is not uncommon in people in her situation; many refugees and survivors felt so-called survivors' guilt, questioning why they had survived while friends and relatives had perished. Ellen felt this very strongly as she was the only one of her siblings who had survived the *Shoah*. Ellen did not feel that she was able to forgive the crimes of the Holocaust, and she was sure that she would never forget them. She spoke very movingly at a conference at Aberystwyth University in July 2016, in front of an international audience including many researchers from Germany, and she contributed to the BBC Wales *Eye on Wales* radio programme on the Kindertransport in 2018, helping to inform public memory of the Holocaust in Wales.

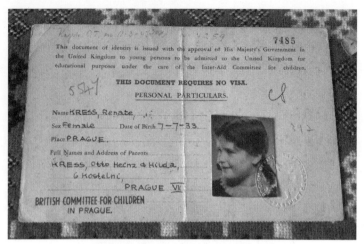

Renate Collins' Kindertransport ID Card
(© Amy Daniel)

Renate Collins family (© Renate Collins)

'MY FIRST CWTCH':
RENATE COLLINS IN PORTH

Renate Collins was one of a number of very young children who were put on a Kindertransport unaccompanied in order to save them from the Nazis. She was born Renate Kress on 7 July 1933, in Prague, and arrived in the UK on 1 July 1939, just days before her sixth birthday. Her story is one of limited recollection of her early life, and a successful integration into a new life in Wales. For years, she only remembered five close family members, who were all murdered in the Holocaust. Later a second cousin who had also fled to the UK managed to uncover details of the fates of 64 members of her extended family. Not one of them had survived the Holocaust.

Renate's father was German by birth and arrived in Prague because his father, Renate's paternal grandfather, took up an appointment at a bank in the city. Renate's father followed in her grandfather's footsteps, and also worked in banking. The family spoke Czech and German. Renate's mother's family were originally from Bohemia, then part of the Habsburg Empire, and Renate has photos showing her in traditional national Bohemian costume. Renate remembers people's reactions to these pictures and – to British eyes – the outlandish-looking costume, which always reminded her that this is where the expression 'bohemian' comes from. During the first five years of her life, Renate grew up as an only child in a family of men and women with outstanding careers: both in business but also in the arts. Her great aunt was a sculptor who worked on official art projects for the Czechoslovak government and had studied for three years with the famous sculptor Auguste Rodin in Paris. Her mother worked as a nurse and continued to do so after Renate was born.

Renate has fond memories of her birth parents, but she remembers them being not very physically affectionate in comparison with her foster parents; she could not remember her birth mother or father kissing or cuddling her. She felt that they were trying to toughen her up to prepare her for life's challenges. Renate also does not recall any toys she played with in Prague. Outdoor pursuits played an important role in her family life. There is a photograph depicting three-year old Renate on skis, and she was given a pair of skates to take with her to Wales, something that no doubt puzzled her foster family as ice-skating was not a common pursuit in the 1930s and 1940s in Wales.

In contrast to Vera Gissing, Renate had no negative memories of the Germans occupying Prague. The German army took over her school's kitchen, but the soldiers were friendly to her. After her nursery day ended, she was supposed to go to her aunt's flat just across the road. She remembered that the Germans gave her sweets and took her hand to help her cross the road and reach the building where her aunt's flat was located. When Renate visited the city of her birth in 1996, after the end of the communist regime in Czechoslovakia, 47 years after leaving Prague as a child, she was surprised that she could still remember her early childhood home, just below the castle, in the Kostelní area of Prague. She recognised her apartment building and her nursery school and the immediate vicinity:

'I said to my husband, "This is near where I used to live." Because there's so many bridges, and I knew I walked down the road, round the corner and there was the bridge. And he went quite quiet, and he said, "I feel quite peculiar, to think, after all these years..." And, of course, when we went to Kostelní, which is where I lived, I was quite right, it had come back to me, because I suppose that was the only part of Prague that I ever went. And then we came down from the castle, and I saw my school, because I used to have to go down to my great aunt's, the sculptress, from school, and then my mother would pick me up.'

Renate's birth parents and her foster parents had corresponded with each other before she left Prague. While many Kindertransportees were only allocated individual foster placements after their arrival, this was different in the case of Renate Collins. This could have been because of her young age, or due to the fact that she fled from Prague. The Kindertransports from Prague were organised slightly differently than those from Germany or Austria. The rescue started after the German invasion of Czechoslovakia in March 1939 and thus later than the Kindertransports from Germany and Austria. Nicholas Winton, who was a young British lawyer and stockbroker at the time, is often associated with this particular part of the Kindertransport rescue scheme; Winton travelled to Prague and became instrumental in organising the rescue of 669 children and teenagers. He became the only well-remembered individual rescuer in Kindertransport history. There are many reasons for this, including his longevity: Winton died in 2015 aged 106. He was also one of the few rescuers still alive in the 21st century when the Kindertransport became more widely recognised by the general public. However, Winton was not the only British person involved in the children's rescue from Czechoslovakia: others included Trevor Chadwick and Doreen Warriner. The British team worked more closely and locally with their Czechoslovak counterparts and there was even more urgency to their mission as clearly the Jewish population had had no time at all to prepare for the imposition of anti-Jewish laws from the German invaders. By March 1939, there were also few of the foster placements and the group guarantees of £50 per child remaining from the initial pool. Both were needed to enable an unaccompanied child refugee to be admitted to the UK on a Kindertransport. The organisers of the Kindertransport from Prague clearly felt that the matter of bringing Jewish children out of Czechoslovakia was very urgent, and so Winton showed photos of individual children to potential foster parents in the UK who could then select a child. While this practice seems highly questionable from a contemporary viewpoint on child protection standards, it meant that foster parents knew the identity of the child they were to host before he or she arrived in the UK.

Renate remembers her departure from Prague and the journey to the UK. She had had chickenpox and a fever, and normally children were not allowed to join a Kindertransport if they were ill. Renate's mother was also reluctant to send her away in this state of ill health but her doctor, whose teenage daughter was put on the same transport, impressed on Renate's mother that there was a danger that she would not get out at all if she did not join this transport in July. As it happened, the doctor was right. The final Kindertransport train from Prague was prevented from leaving on 3 September 1939 as war had already started. Renate remembers lying down on the journey, sleeping a lot of the time and not feeling entirely well. When she arrived in London, she was met by her foster father, a Baptist minister. He was dressed in a black hat and coat, wore a black suit and a minister's collar, and smiled at her. Renate took his hand and went with him, and they went by train to Wales. Renate had a wicker case with some clothes and her skates with her; she remembered it feeling very heavy.

Renate's foster parents were Sidney and Arianwen Coplestone, who lived in Porth and had no biological children. Sidney was the minister of the Baptist Church in Porth. The couple had met at theological college. Arianwen was an educated woman and a Welsh speaker; she carried out duties beyond the ones typical for a minister's wife of the time, including conducting Welsh-language sermons. Renate's birth parents exchanged letters and photographs with her foster parents. This even included statements from Renate herself that her birth mother had included in the letters sent to her foster parents. Renate said that she was going to be a good girl if she did not have to eat spinach and if she could have ice cream. When Renate arrived at the home of her foster family, she was overwhelmed by the affection that her foster mother showed her. She recalled getting her 'first Welsh cwtch' and kiss. She did not remember her birth parents being so physically affectionate.

Arianwen undid Renate's plaits and washed her hair; she decided to leave Renate's hair loose as she found her ringlets adorable. Sidney was also very good with children, as he had a lot of contact with children and young people due to his ministry, his teaching and visiting members of his congregation.

When Renate woke up on the Sunday morning after her arrival in Porth, she looked into the face of another little girl. This girl was Pat Evans (later Pat Warren) and she and Renate became lifelong friends. They were still in close contact in 2021. Renate went to church with her new foster parents and enjoyed collecting hymn books after the service together with other little girls. Over the next weeks and months, Renate received a lot of attention from members of the congregation and the local community. Three babies born into the congregation after her arrival were named Renate; these name choices were definitely inspired by her arrival as the name had been virtually unknown in the local area before then.

The integration of a Jewish child into a Christian community as happened with Renate might look questionable to us today. There were some concerns at the time about proselytising and not respecting religious differences, and this worried some organisers of the Kindertransport more than others. As noted above, many argued that saving lives must take priority over such considerations. There were not enough foster families with a Jewish background in the UK, as the UK Jewish population was small, counting only around 350,000 by the start of the Second World War. It was clearly impossible for such a small community to provide foster placements for so many children in such a short space of time. Living with families who had a different religious background caused problems for the relationships between some child refugees and their foster parents, but this often depended on individual circumstances.

In this case of Renate and the Coplestones, the integration of a small child into the lives of her foster parents was an organic process. There was no deliberate attempt to alienate her from her religious background. In fact, Sidney was very interested in inter-faith relations and later lectured on Jewish-Christian relations at Swansea University. Renate's foster parents wanted her to retain her religious identity and as an adult, Renate identified as Jewish.

The Coplestones received a constant stream of visitors to their flat of parishioners wanting to discuss funerals, weddings, or other church business. For the purpose of meeting the members of the congregation in the home, the family had to keep the front room tidy at all times. This room was only used for special occasions and visitors. Renate started to bring cups of tea to the visitors, which kept her busy and made her feel useful. There was no outside space attached to the flat, which Renate missed as her birth family had enjoyed the outdoors and sport very much.

Renate liked helping around the house, and especially enjoyed cooking. While she was still in the early years of primary school, her foster mother became ill and had a lengthy stay in hospital. A local teacher came to stay at the Coplestone's flat, because Arianwen did not like the idea of Sidney being alone in the house with their foster daughter. She was worried that people would talk about this and say, 'Oh ... Sidney's there with a little girl in the house on his own.' When the teacher went to the hospital one day to visit Arianwen, she said, 'Well, I've never been so embarrassed in my life, I had to have a seven-year-old tell me how to make gravy!'

Initially Renate could only say 'yes' or 'no' in English, and she was later unsure whether she actually knew the meaning of the words and used them in the correct way. Yet, Renate clearly learnt English quickly. She had to go to school in September and, in those days, there would have been no English support lessons or teaching assistants to help her. Sidney was very keen on English grammar, so Renate ended up in being one of the best students in the subject when she entered senior school.

Renate also grew up with the Welsh language although she never learnt to speak it fluently. The first year she went to senior school, Welsh lessons were part of the curriculum. Arianwen was originally from Fishguard and was a Welsh speaker. She preached in Welsh, and a lot of people in her community were first language Welsh speakers. After her first year of learning Welsh at school, Renate was put in the German class. But she came bottom of the class. Renate wondered that there must have been emotional reasons why she was unable to recover her German or learn it anew. Renate forgot her Czech, too, as she never had anyone to speak it with. She also wondered whether she wanted to subconsciously suppress her past. Not thinking about her past would spare her pain:

> 'I wanted to obliterate my past. Not intentionally, I didn't think, but [the teacher] said, "it might have been that", so they put me in the third year, in the Latin class and I did quite well there.'

Renate's birth parents and her foster parents corresponded with each other for the first few months after she arrived and before the war broke out. Renate has little recollection of this but has some correspondence in her possession. For some reason, she recalled an occasion where her foster father was really annoyed that her birth parents had not sent her with a straw hat, and he communicated this in a letter. In later life, Renate reflected on this, and felt that it was very odd to be annoyed about such a thing, bearing in mind the extreme circumstances of little Renate's flight and arrival. Renate received only one last communication from her family after the Second World War broke out: this was a so-called Red Cross postcard from her mother, who was by then incarcerated in a concentration camp. The card was sent on the occasion of Renate's birthday in 1942. It was dated 10 June 1942, and read:

> 'Many happy birthday wishes, we think continually of you. Are well, hope you too. Much love, kind regards and thanks to your foster parents.'

Despite her young age, Renate did not forget her birth parents. During the war years, she still believed she would be going back to

Czechoslovakia after the war. This was not a detailed thought but an emotional feeling.

Renate only discovered the exact circumstances of her mother's death as late as October 2021. Her mother's death certificate, which she had seen much earlier, noted her mother's place of death as Treblinka. This was in fact incorrect: her mother and her grandmother were deported and on the way to Treblinka concentration camp when the train broke down. Rather than waiting for the train to be repaired, the guards shot all the deportees. Renate never heard from her father, but she found out after 1945 that he and her uncle, Felix, had been murdered in Auschwitz. Her mother, grandmother, father and uncle were all killed roughly at the same time in 1944. Renate only found out the time of their deaths after 1996, when she finally returned to Prague. (She had been advised not to travel to her former home country while the Communist regime was still in power.) Although Renate uncovered the details of her parents' deaths much, much later she had been informed of their murder soon after the end of the Second World War. After learning of their deaths, Sidney and Arianwen adopted Renate – in 1947 when she was 14 years old. By then she had spent nine years in Porth. Renate was devastated that her parents were dead. Her devastation led her to hang on to the irrational thought that this might in fact be not true and there might still be a chance of a reunion. Because everything was so chaotic in Europe at the end of the war, she managed to hang on to the hope that her birth parents might be found later. At the same time, she felt accepted in Porth and she felt that she was treated like everyone else:

> 'But when you're fourteen years old, and you've spent nine years where you actually are, the past, I mean I was very sad, obviously that I'd lost my mother and my father, but in a way, most of my life had been in Wales. And at one time, when Lisl said they were dead, I thought "Oh, perhaps, you know, they might find them

later on." But no, I was accepted, I was treated like everybody else, you know.'

Renate did not know who had brought her over to the UK and how the Kindertransport had worked, neither did her adoptive father fully understand, until she was asked to appear on a TV show in 1988. The show was called *That's Life* and was broadcast by the BBC. in this particular episode, the well-known presenter Esther Rantzen presented Nicholas Winton with the story of his life. Winton had no idea that the part of his life when he rescued children from Prague would feature on the programme. He was sitting in the studio surrounded by about 100 people who turned out to be former child refugees who had fled on a Kindertransport from Prague. It is a very emotional scene when Esther Rantzen reveals this to Nicholas Winton and all the former child refugees around him stand up.

Renate does not recall experiencing much bullying, antisemitism or racism. She experienced the solidarity of a close-knit community. There were over thirty coal mines in her valley, and mining was a dangerous job. Every month or so, someone would get killed in an accident down the mines, and these tragedies and other challenges of this difficult working life brought people closer and they worried less about people's ethnicity or religion. Despite being a refugee, Renate's experience of bullying was not so different from many other children's: she defended a boy once who was bullied and beaten up at school, and she argued with a girl who was distantly related to her family because she was bullying others. As a teenager, Renate joined in with a small group of eight or nine youngsters from the Baptist church. The friends spent a lot of time together and went rambling and for picnics. They gave each other support and this helped Renate with puberty worries.

Life with her foster parents was quite constrained, but she did not feel she ever wanted for anything. Although she was successful at secondary school, she left before gaining qualifications, which she felt a little sad about. Her parents demanded quite a high level of participation in household chores from her which interfered with her schooling and hobbies like hockey. After leaving school, she attended a local commercial college and studied accountancy, typing and shorthand. Her adoptive father then informed her he could no longer afford to keep her. Renate recalls in an interview:

'And the year that I was in commercial college, my adoptive dad said, "I can't afford to keep you, you've got to go out to work." So I went to work, and I was trying to do my course evenings, but I was going to Cardiff quarter to seven in the morning, coming back half past six at night, and I just couldn't go to college seven o'clock till nine o'clock. So I gave it up, but I got a very good job in BOAC, in Treforest, which is now British Airways, and I was there till I was married.'

This clearly was a very good job and Renate was happy about earning money.

The Coplestones used to host some long-time visitors, for example, people who spoke or preached in the local vicinity. One such speaker stayed for a week, and then invited the family to her guesthouse in Cornwall in return. Sidney, Arianwen and Renate stayed for three weeks, and during this stay the woman asked Renate whether she would like to visit her brother's farm. Renate was keen, and there she met David, her future husband, for the first time. The two families stayed in touch and when, two years later, David was doing his military service at the air force base in St Athan, the Coplestones invited him to their home. Renate and David became a couple. They married in 1954 in Cornwall and then lived there for 47 years. The couple had two sons: Paul, who was born in 1958, and Peter, who was born in 1960. Renate's husband sold farm machinery for a living, and Renate worked in the hospitality industry. She felt that David's family welcomed and accepted her, and she became close to many of them. She did, of course, have no close blood relatives of her own; however, she stayed close to her adoptive parents and visited them frequently. When they did so, Renate and David always dropped in on her friends in Porthcawl and especially on her old friend Pat and her family.

In 2001, David and Renate moved to Wales after their retirement. David died in 2007. Renate has spent a lot of time in recent years visiting schools and contributing to Holocaust education. In 2020, she was awarded a BEM for services to Holocaust education. Over the years, Renate has met Tony Blair and Prince Charles. In 2022, she was one of the last surviving refugees who had fled National Socialism and resettled in Wales.

Tree felling by Alien Pioneers, 1943 (© IWM H27260) –
At the mill. Pte. Morganstein watches the first cut. Pte.
Morganstein is an Austrian and used to run his own
clothiers business.

Shoulder Badge, No. 10 (Inter-Allied) Commando
(© IWM INS 8101)

'DIGGING FOXHOLES IN CARMARTHENSHIRE': HERBERT PATRICK ANDERSON AND THE PIONEER CORPS

Many refugees were willing to fight actively against National Socialism. Some were prepared to do so in the Armed Forces. This was, however, not an entirely straightforward process. Before the Second World War, refugees had not been allowed to join the British Army at all. The authorities had doubts as to the refugees' loyalty to their country of sanctuary. After the first few months of the Second World War, a non-combative unit was formed: the Pioneer Corps was to be made up of friendly aliens. Later, other possibilities opened up. Herbert Anderson joined the Pioneer Corps and spent over 18 months in Wales with his Pioneer Corps unit.

Herbert Anderson had been born Helmut Herbert Fürst on 16 April 1913 in Berlin. His parents were Austrian citizens, and his father had moved around Europe several times in connection with his work in the field of paraffin production. The couple were living in Berlin when their eldest son was born, but soon after Herbert's birth, at the beginning of the First World War, they returned to Austria, because his father had been drafted into the Austrian Army. Herbert's mother was from a Jewish family and Herbert's father also had some Jewish ancestry but had been brought up in the Christian tradition.

Herbert had some memories of his childhood during the First World War. He later recalled that his family always had one or two maids and that they changed employment a lot. He remembered different maids being very upset because their boyfriends had been killed in the war. His mother's four brothers had all served in the Austrian army, as well as his own father, and fortunately they all survived.

Herbert started school at six years old in 1919. He went to a primary school that was attached to a teacher training college, with the consequence that it had very high academic standards. Children were required to draw maps in the first and the second year. Trainee teachers were always sitting at the back of the class observing the lessons. Herbert loved this school. At 11 he sat an exam and, as he did well, he was admitted to a good grammar school in Vienna. It was the same school that the Austrian composer Franz Schubert had attended in the early 19th century.

By the 1920s, Herbert's father was working for an American firm. Herbert later recalled that some tensions developed between them: his father was a staunch supporter of a capitalist market economy. By contrast, twelve-year-old Herbert was already a member of the left-wing youth organisation, the Red Falcons. He was also a member of the Boy Scouts movement and, in the summer of 1929, his Viennese group travelled to England to a Scout Jamboree in Birkenhead. On the journey, they stopped for a night at Verdun and explored the historic sites of the First World War, which left an impression on Herbert. The jamboree in England was less successful as it poured with rain for three days in Birkenhead. The leader of Herbert's troop declared after the third day that enough was enough and they took down the tents and went to London, which Herbert liked very much. This was his first encounter with the UK.

Herbert later recalled that students of Jewish origin were treated more harshly than others, but he also remembered the beginning of a more progressive education policy during his time at school. A Jewish boy had written something rude about a teacher on the blackboard and was immediately expelled, which was obviously a very harsh punishment. The boy was so upset he climbed to the top of the school building, jumped off, and killed himself. After this tragic incident, the regime became more progressive, in tune with a wider progressive movement in Austria, and especially in Vienna. However, after the civil war in 1934, all this came to an end and Austrofascism was established. Herbert's family became increasingly worried throughout these years, and their fears were realised in 1938, when National Socialist Germany annexed Austria.

On the evening of 11 March 1938, Herbert was at his uncle's flat for a Friday night evening meal when they heard German planes circling over Vienna, the prelude to the annexation. Herbert later recalled how the Austrians greeted the Germans as if they were liberators. He was one of the 200,000 who went to hear Hitler's speech on the Heldenplatz. The week after the speech, there were 300 suicides in Vienna, including many Jewish people who felt that this was the end for them. Herbert heard the constant false allegations made against Austrian Jews and saw Jewish people dragged out of their flats and put into police vans. He had spoken to many German Jewish refugees, and they had all impressed on him the need to get out. His parents were more reluctant and told him to organise it himself if he was so keen for them to leave. Herbert decided to get them all to the UK, where they had previously enjoyed two wonderful holidays on the Isle of Wight. By June 1938, the family had managed to find someone to guarantee that his parents would not become a burden to the British taxpayer.

Herbert was working in Istanbul that winter, where he was nearly arrested over a dispute as to whether his Austrian passport was still valid as technically Austria did not exist anymore. Fortunately, he was well connected, and the Austrian Consul managed to get the British Consul to grant Herbert a permit for entry into the UK. He also obtained a ticket on a cargo ship to Hull and made the journey to England. He had been able to save much of his salary in Istanbul and arrived in the UK with £330 – a large sum of money at the time. This was fortunate because Herbert's employment prospects in the UK were not good. The only two options open to him were working as a nursing assistant in a psychiatric hospital or as a farm labourer. He opted for the latter and ended up on a farm near Shaftesbury. He was treated well, but only received one pound pocket money per week for his labour. The local young women liked him and he was often asked where he was from. When he answered Austria, they thought he meant Australia. When he corrected them, they had never heard of the Central European country.

Both Herbert and his father felt that the only way to get rid of the National Socialist poison in Europe was a victorious war. Hence once war was declared, Herbert's next mission was to rid himself of his status as an enemy alien. He understood that it was difficult for the UK authorities to distinguish between refugees and non-refugees, and to some extent between enemy aliens and friendly aliens. He prepared well for his tribunal and knew that to prove his case he would have to bring testimonials from people who had got to know him in UK. In the end, he brought three letters: one from his employer on the farm, one from a well-regarded local man of about 55 who was blind and with whom he had become friends, and one from a Mr Baker who had been helped by his family in the First World War when Baker, a member of the Quaker faith, had been interned in Vienna. Herbert was declared a 'friendly alien' and was therefore able to move around freely in the UK.

The next step for Herbert was to try and join any part of the Armed Forces that would have him and which might be mobilised against Hitler's regime. His employer was not very happy that Herbert was trying to leave as he had already lost five male employees, who had been called up, and he had only two female employees left besides Herbert. He offered the young man a proper farm labourer's wage of £2.15 per week. This was tempting but Herbert wanted to do something more radical. He was given a letter of introduction to the recruitment officer of a Guards regiment but because of Herbert's foreign background they would not consider him, and his first attempt to join up failed. He then received a letter from the refugee organisation headquarters at Woburn House in London, informing him that an international unit, something similar to the French Foreign Legion, was about to be established. In the end, the Pioneer Corps turned out not to be quite so glamorous, set up as a non-combative unit for the purpose of assisting ordinary military units.

Herbert was called up to join the Pioneer Corps early in 1940. He had spent a few weeks, including Christmas, with his parents in London, where he listened to the King's first wartime Christmas address, which he thought was very moving.

On 12 February 1940, he arrived at a training camp in Richborough in Kent. The winter was extremely cold, and the men were accommodated in wooden huts that had stood empty since they had accommodated German prisoners during the First World War. In his company at that time, there were a small number of regular British soldiers and 200 friendly aliens. At Herbert's estimate, about 60 per cent were German, about 25 per cent were Austrian and the remaining 15 per cent were other nationalities. He thought that about 70 per cent of his unit in the Pioneer Corps were Jewish. Among these men he made some very close friends, including his best friend – a man he would still phone every other day over 50 years later. The unit also included 20 to 30 men who had served in the First World War as there was no age limit for the Pioneer Corps.

Herbert was quickly made a corporal because his sergeant felt that his ability to speak fluent French would be useful. Herbert's company was one of the first to be sent to France, where they were deployed in Le Havre to work as dockers. They helped units of the British Expeditionary Force (BEF) off boats and unloaded equipment. It was the time of the so-called phoney war and things still seemed very peaceful; however, this would not last. After Germany invaded Belgium on 10 May 1940, things quickly went badly for the Allies and Herbert's company was first commanded to get out of Belgium and then, shortly afterwards, commanded to get out of France by any means they could find. They had trucks and they moved west towards Nantes and Roscoff. Herbert felt that the French population stopped being friendly towards them now as they felt that the British were abandoning them. The desperate journey turned into a bit of an odyssey and the company ended up near Saint-Malo, where they camped on a racecourse. There were no French ships in the harbour, but they did find a British coal cargo ship that still had its load in the hull and was being turned back to Britain.

At this point, on 17 June 1940, it was already 13 days since the end of the Dunkirk evacuation, and there was unlikely to be any other means of exiting France for the Pioneers if they could not get on this ship. The skipper of coal boat refused to take them, as he thought they would be overloaded with both the cargo and the Pioneers. However, when they agreed to leave their rifles and other equipment behind them, he changed his mind and let them on board. The returning Pioneers arrived to a rapturous welcome from the locals in Weymouth, where they docked, despite or possibly because of the fact that they were covered in coal dust. The local population gave them flowers and chocolates, and their Cockney officer made a speech claiming that they were men who were willing to give their lives for Britain. In this way, Herbert's Pioneer Corps had its own Dunkirk-type escape.

A new period of training and constant moving about ensued. They were re-equipped in Bideford in Devon, where they undertook the heavy and dangerous task of excavating bombs that the Luftwaffe had dropped in Somerset, especially around Ilminster and Taunton. They were now called the 87th Company Pioneer Corps and moved on to a brief stint in London, helping out observatory units and undertaking duties which included entering buildings that had been bombed and removing the dead. After this period of duty in London, Herbert's company was told it was being moved to Wales for recuperation. Herbert was in the advance unit and later remembered arriving in Felindre in Carmarthenshire and finding the river Teifi, with its coracles, incredibly peaceful. This time, his stay in Wales did not last long, as the company were soon told that they were to be moved to Liverpool. There, for the first time, Herbert saw anti-war demonstrations. He remembers these being small, and he thought that they were ridiculous because to his mind only a successful war could restore peace and an acceptable way of life to the Continent.

In June 1941, Herbert's company's 18-month stay in South Wales began. The men were split up into smaller units and his was billeted at East Blockhouse in Pembrokeshire. The area was very pretty, and their quarters overlooked the sea. Their duties included carrying ammunition for the Royal Artillery in Manorbier. While stationed in Pembrokeshire, Herbert felt he got to know many small places in South and Mid Wales, though he never travelled any further north than Aberaeron.

While at the Pembroke Docks barracks, the men of the Pioneer Corps received further training. One day, Geoffrey Garrett, a well-known journalist and pacifist, was training them to defuse a landmine. Tragically, on this occasion, the training went badly wrong and Garrett and 19 men, including three German Jewish refugees, died in an explosion. Eight men from Herbert's unit were among the dead, but fortunately he had been carrying out other duties away from the barracks on that day. The funeral was a big occasion and all the coffins were wrapped in Union Jacks but Herbert later recalled wondering what the coffins actually contained as the explosion had been devastating.

After the accident, Herbert was put in charge of 20 men and assigned the task of digging 'foxholes' in Carmarthenshire. This involved digging a hole into which could be sunk a wooden 'kiosk' with a seat, just about big enough for a man to conceal himself within. These would be connected by a telephone line and were intended to form a communication network should there be a German invasion. Herbert felt that this was a completely ridiculous idea:

'We had the most ridiculous task. We were to dig holes in the soil all over the county. And wondering why? Who would envisage an invasion of Britain via Carmarthenshire? [...] I am still wondering whether the holes are still all over Carmarthenshire today?'

All the men asked themselves who in their right mind could possibly imagine that the German army would choose to invade Britain via South Wales, as opposed to crossing the mere 22 miles of English Channel from France to Kent.

There are many stories that show that the work of the Pioneer Corps had an air of 'Dad's Army' about it and this was recognised by the former refugees at the time. Some, therefore, refused to join the Corps, as we will see from Harry Weinberger's story (p. 224). Others, such as Herbert, made the most of their time in the Corps, even if the work could be frustrating occasionally. They had no mechanical equipment to carry out the task of digging the foxholes, just their spades, and so they dug, spadeful by spadeful, rain or shine.

Herbert certainly loved his time in Wales. He felt that the locals treated all the Pioneers well, and that it was no disadvantage being a continental foreigner. When he was hitchhiking in Wales, he would often get lifts from local farmers. When they asked him about his accent, and he said that he was from Austria, the reply often was, 'You're not from England? Oh, that's all right then.'

Herbert liked music and played the piano and when a local man heard him play on an inferior instrument in the canteen, the man invited him to his home to play on a good piano. Herbert accepted this invitation and subsequently, Jack Morgan, a chemist whose family lived above his shop, and Herbert became good friends. The family were Welsh speakers and Herbert liked that as it gave him more insight into the society of his host country. Herbert remembers: 'They were very Welsh – and I liked that. They spoke Welsh in the family, even when I was there. I did not mind that.'

Herbert got invited to supper frequently, and to play the piano. He became godfather to Jack's daughter. Being friends with Jack also introduced Herbert to another aspect of local life, the non-conformist Welsh chapel. Jack played the organ at the chapel, but what interested Herbert most was the political and educational aspect of chapel life. Herbert remembered listening to many lectures that helped him understand the political and social life in Wales and the question, 'Once the war is over, what will the country do for a different future?'

Eventually Herbert's unit was moved to Haverfordwest, and then once more to Aberaeron. Herbert loved Aberaeron 'with its whole square full of genuine Georgian houses'. Aberaeron always had a special place in his heart because his future wife Kathleen visited him in the town. He'd met her in London, and they got to know each other quickly. She undertook a difficult journey to the town, having decided to visit Herbert, especially since it was against general advice to travel without absolutely compelling reasons. They spent an idyllic week in Aberaeron, and eleven months later, on 7 August 1943, the couple were married.

In the meantime, Herbert had been approached by a superior officer and asked whether he was interested in joining a special operations unit. Herbert was keen to do so and he was called to London where he was sworn to secrecy. He was asked which area of Austria he knew best and answered the Tyrolese Austrian mountains, as he did not want to go back to Vienna during hostilities. At the beginning of 1944, he was moved to Hampshire to start his training which was extremely arduous. He was tested on his language skills and passed that part with flying colours. He had more trouble regarding his parachute skills as he injured his foot during one landing and had to repeat the training. He was part of a small group of men who were to be dropped by parachute behind enemy lines and who would then try and carry out acts of sabotage and cause as much damage as they could to the enemy.

After a few weeks training in mechanical sabotage, he ended up at Anderson barracks near Wimbourne in Dorset. The men in his unit were asked to change their Teutonic-sounding names for more English-sounding ones. It was feared that an Allied soldier with a German name would be immediately shot as a traitor if captured by the enemy. Herbert pondered a number of possible new surnames and ran them past Kathleen. Unfortunately, they did not come up with an acceptable idea and so, when he was asked the next

215

day, he could only think of the name of the barracks. This is how he ended up with the name Herbert Anderson.

In 1944, the members of the special operations unit were told they could be sent to the Continent any day; however, nothing had happened by the time Herbert's son Robert was born on 2 May 1944. On hearing of his son's birth, Herbert immediately asked for compassionate leave but this was denied. His commanding officer was annoyed by the request and asked Herbert which was more important to him, his family or the army. When Herbert answered that his family was more important to him, he was transferred to a different unit. This was the end of his career in special operations. He thus escaped a risky mission. One of his friends who was dropped in Austria, and tried to work undercover in Vienna, was discovered and sent to Mauthausen concentration camp.

However, Herbert did make it back to the Continent in the uniform of a member of the British Forces later in the war. He became part of a so-called civil affairs unit attached to the Canadian Army. He entered Germany as part of the final offensive on one of the specially built bridges across the Rhine. Herbert saw some serious fighting and was very traumatised by the sight of all the dead bodies of Germans who had been hung for desertion in the last few days of war.

Herbert found himself close to where the final surrender was signed on 8 May 1945. His unit's first job was to prevent Nazis from crossing over the border to Denmark to evade capture – a futile task as they had no way of telling who had been a Nazi and who had not. They also had to help the German authorities cope with the large influx of Germans fleeing from the former eastern territories and the difficulties this was causing local communities.

Eventually, Herbert's unit was stationed in Eutin and his skills as an interpreter were much in demand. He was the only German speaker in his unit and Herbert remembered never working so hard again in his whole life. He would be called day and night to interpret between the local population, the German authorities, and the military authorities. Many Germans told him that they had not been Nazis and he never replied sarcastically, 'Of course, you were not', though it was tempting to do so.

Herbert's son Robert Anderson would later become a renowned museum curator and historian of science. He became the director of the British Museum from 1992 to 2002.

Harry Weinberger.
Screenshot from AJR Refugee Voices Testimony
Archive interview, 10 March 2005. Courtesy of
Association of Jewish Refugees (© AJR)

Family photos of Harry Weinberger.
Courtesy of Harry Weinberger's personal archive and
Association of Jewish Refugees (© AJR)

'LADDY, THAT CAN BE ARRANGED': HARRY WEINBERGER'S ADVENTUROUS LIFE STORY

To find the stories of refugees from National Socialism who settled in Wales, I have researched both public archives and private collections of papers. Other information has come from former refugees telling their life stories in interviews and memoirs. In my decades-long research career, I have learnt that different individuals tell their stories in very different ways, influenced by many factors such as their personality, their communication style, their class and educational background, their gender, and, above all, the stage of life at which the interview is given. Harry Weinberger was a gentle storyteller, but he nevertheless gives his life the air of an adventure. As a young man, he was keen on physically fighting against the Nazis, and he eventually fought in the British army against fascist Italy.

Harry Weinberger was born in Berlin on 7 April 1924 into a non-religious Jewish family. He had an older brother called Bernd, and a younger sister called Ina. His family never went to a synagogue and he did not receive any Jewish religious instruction, but some of his relatives were interested in Zionism. When, as a young boy, he asked his father whether there was a god, his father answered 'no', something that stuck permanently in Harry's mind. His father was a wealthy businessman who owned a factory. The family lived in a large flat with a view of the river Spree, and the children were looked after by nannies and tutors. When the family went on holiday, the children travelled separately from their parents: they went to the North German seaside with their nanny or tutor, and their parents went abroad on their own. Harry remembered some details about the events of February 1933, immediately after the Nazis rose to power:

> 'We had a, what do you call them, porter, concierge, called Fölzmann in the house and in February 1933 he turned up in full Nazi uniform, which was a bit of a surprise. When the Reichstag burned, I saw from our windows the glow in the sky and heard the fire engines and was very aware what had happened politically. But like many others we thought it would all be over soon.'

The Reichstag building, seat of the German Parliament, was destroyed on 27 February 1933, and Harry was able to see the glow emanating from the burning Reichstag in the Berlin sky and hear the fire engines in the streets. The Nazi leadership and its coalition partners claimed that Communists were behind the arson attack and that they were planning a violent uprising. The Nazis claimed that emergency legislation was needed to prevent this. Such legislation was introduced swiftly and this decree abolished a number of constitutional protections and paved the way for establishing a Nazi dictatorship.

Although Weinberger's father was one of the German Jewish citizens who thought the Nazis would not last long, he decided to move the family out of Germany until the Nazis had been removed from power, which he expected to happen within weeks. As he had business connections and the means to afford the relocation, he moved the family to Český Těšín in Czechoslovakia in 1933:

'... when the grown-ups said that we would leave Germany I was very upset and I remember walking through the streets near my home, trying to memorise them, I didn't know how long it would be until I'd see them again.'

Harry had witnessed the street fighting in Germany between right-wing and left-wing groups, and he remembered Hitler's public speeches as those of a madman who made no sense, and his audiences as a crazed mass shouting '*Sieg Heil*'. In comparison, life in Czechoslovakia initially seemed free and easy, and he felt that they had found a second home. He found learning Czech difficult, but nevertheless learnt it quickly, and managed to pass the entry exam for secondary school in Czech, which pleased him. As Harry grew older and his knowledge of recent history and contemporary politics increased, he felt more and more strongly that he needed to take action. He learnt about the civil war in Spain, and very much regretted that he was not old enough to go to Spain and fight. By 1937, he felt he knew what the Nazis had done, and wanted everyone to know. But the atmosphere in Czechoslovakia was not always one of solidarity with the victims of National Socialism. There were also tensions between the different groups of refugees. The earlier refugees had been able to bring some of their money and assets to Czechoslovakia and felt resentful that they were expected to look after those Austrian refugees who had nothing but the clothes on their backs when they fled. While living in Czechoslovakia, the family's economic situation had deteriorated as Mr Weinberger was not allowed to work. The family's furniture, jewellery and library slowly disappeared. When Germany finally invaded Czechoslovakia, Harry witnessed firsthand the violence and cruelty of the new rulers, especially the violence of the Austrian SS troops; he saw the brutality of the Nazi regime for himself and recognised that the country had fallen into a lawless state where there was no authority, justice or police authority. Jews could be hounded. People just disappeared. Harry felt that his parents, or adult authority figures in general, would not be able to protect him. Hence, aged 15, Harry joined a group of young people who helped people flee to Hungary. He did not tell his family; his father did not approve of any illegal activity. Nor did he tell his parents about getting into street fights, being injured by and injuring members of the local Hitler Youth.

Harry's escape on the Kindertransport was due to luck rather than foresight. Only his younger sister had the correct papers for the transport. Harry had been tasked with taking her to the station... By summer 1939, it must have been clear to many that escape routes such as the Kindertransport might not remain open for long. The organisers of the Kindertransports from Prague were less strict about staying with the realms of 'legality' – that is keeping to the rules imposed on the scheme by the Nazis. All Kindertransport trains had accompanying adult guardians who would often be teachers or social workers. These guardians were not allowed to stay in the UK but had to return to the country the trains had come from. However, when an acquaintance saw Harry at the station and noticed that only Ina had a visa, he offered Harry a place as accompanying adult and this – although clearly against the rules – got Harry to the UK:

> 'An official, who I knew because we had been skiing together, got out of the train, which stood ready to leave, and gave me one of those things you put on your arm which said Reisebegleiter [travelling companion] the man who accompanies the children and told me to hop on, and I had nothing with me, and my sister had a little suitcase. My sister was about 10 years old, and we said goodbye to my parents and got onto the train.'

It is not quite clear how he obtained the correct papers after his arrival in the UK, but the fact that his grandparents were already UK residents and that he was only 15 must have helped.

Harry remembers that quite a lot of the children on the train were terrified; all the train stations they passed had men in uniform gathering on platforms, and military music blaring through the loudspeakers. He remembers the German border guards taunting them and checking them closely in case they had any money or valuables on them, or in their luggage, which was forbidden. Of course, the fact that all these young children had just said goodbye to their parents to set out on a journey into the unknown did not help. Many of the younger children neither quite understood the point of the journey nor had any idea what awaited them at their destination. Given the date he left and his departure point, Harry must have been on the same Kindertransport train as five-year old Renate (p. 195). In fact, Harry remembered that there were many very small children on the train and that he lifted some of them into the luggage racks of the train where they could sleep as if lying in a hammock. Harry felt relieved when he left Prague, despite having to part from his parents. His run-ins with the Hitler Youth and the brutality on the streets must have given him an idea of what was to come. His younger sister was very traumatised by the separation from their parents, and years later underwent therapy to cope with feeling that her parents had abandoned her and sent her away.

Harry was lucky to escape on that last Kindertransport train. Still, Britain came as a bit of a culture shock despite the fact that he was an adventurous teenager. On arrival, he ended up in a hostel in Finsbury Park. This ties in with the memory of other teenagers who were placed in settings that were inappropriate – bearing in mind that they were under-age. Harry was taken to the cinema by some older refugees, and he thought that this was amazing but also a little crazy, especially when between the two main programmes the cinema organ came up from below the floor, words appeared on the screen and everyone started singing.

Once in the UK, Harry had the support of his Koppel grandparents, mentioned in the earlier chapter on the Koppel family, and his stint in the hostel in London did not last long. However, his grandparents clearly had no time to personally care for him and he was immediately sent to boarding school: first in Northamptonshire then to Amersham College in Buckinghamshire. At Amersham, Harry taught himself to paint in oil; he had a lot of time for practising his art and was very productive, especially since he had no parents to go home to in the school holidays. His parents had escaped to Switzerland, but obviously he could not travel to see them. Harry said he felt guilty doing this while other people were fighting in the war:

> 'The war meant that the rest of the world, for whatever reason, were opposed to the Nazis and tried to stop them, and I was very guilty that I wasn't in the war...'

In fact, he tells many stories of trying to be somehow more use to the war effort or attempting to join the army. He tried to join the merchant navy but was rejected on account of his German passport. He did not want to join the Pioneer Corps because he felt that they were a 'ridiculous outfit'; he wanted to join the 'real' British Army.

Harry left school in 1941 and started work in his uncle's factory on the Treforest Estate, remaining there until 1944. This was Harry's introduction to industrial production and working-class life, which felt alien to such a middle-class and privately educated young man. The noise from the hundreds of machines was overwhelming. Initially he operated just one machine, making the same movements over and over again. He felt he produced tiny pieces but did not know to what end. Later, he had to make machines that made the smallest type of mortar. This experience and knowledge proved useful when he was successful in joining the army and his company was asked to dismantle and reassemble mortars; Harry was able to do this quickly and without instruction, and his fellow soldiers thought he was some kind of technical genius. He never let on why he was so good at it.

He also learnt a lot about the hard life of the workers and how little time they had between working, eating, sleeping and then working again. He was surprised by their promiscuous behaviour and by the boisterous and crude jokes of the men. His fellow workers also played a number of practical jokes on him, including one which resulted in him receiving an electric shock. It must have been a big change from being looked after in Berlin by nannies, in Prague by his parents, and even being cared for at his private school. He usually worked ten- hour days with half-an-hour for lunch. Harry had a deal with his landlord that he got a sandwich to take to work and he brewed tea at the factory. As he was a trainee tool maker, the work he did was war work. Nevertheless, he tried again and again to join the active fight against National Socialism.

Being well-educated, and probably also because of his family connection, Harry was given time-off from his usual duties to attend an engineering course. He completed the first year but did not enjoy it. Instead of going to engineering classes, he secretly went to Cardiff School of Art in the evenings without telling the factory managers who, of course, expected him to come back as a qualified engineer.

During those years working and studying in Wales, Harry had a girlfriend for the first time. She was called Eve Evans and worked as an inspector at the nearby aircraft factory. He met her at a party and clumsily approached her, simply saying that he would like her to be his girlfriend. Eve lived in a village outside Pontypridd and, when they had any time off work, Harry and Eve would go walking in the hills, stopping at abandoned villages and buildings. Harry felt very close to Eve but knew he still wanted to join the army. He recalled later:

'We would go for endless walks in the hills without saying much… we were so close and I felt very bad that I did want to join the army and she was going to wait for me and I felt so guilty about her that I never saw her again when I joined up. We were on the closest terms possible but we never communicated again… I behaved fairly badly to her.'

When he had first moved to Wales and started working at the factory, Harry had a lot of trouble finding lodgings. Some members of the local population were very suspicious of him because he was a refugee from Germany. At one of his lodgings, he had a visit from his cousin Heinz Koppel. Of course, they spoke German with each other and – with their common interest in art – they also went out together on trips drawing the local landscape. This aroused suspicion from some of Harry's neighbours, and a sergeant of the Home Guard tried to arrest them. The two men refused to go with him, and clearly this member of the Home Guard was not able to force two rebellious youngsters to do anything. Harry and Heinz simply said that they didn't want to be arrested and went to the fish and chip shop instead. This anecdote is one of the stories that reveals the cheeky nature of his character, and the rebellious narrative he likes to repeat. The sergeant came back with members of the local constabulary and took their names. Apparently, there was a court case – and Harry's landlord was fined for not following proper procedure regarding letting rooms to potential enemy aliens. The fact that they had been making drawings of the local landscape was considered especially suspicious. Their drawings were confiscated and, years later, Harry wondered whether they might still be sitting in a local police archive somewhere in South Wales. Harry had more luck with his next lodging. The landlord was a local miner called Evans who loved music and who had a son called Hayden named after the composer Haydn. One of the conditions for getting the room was to help Hayden with his homework. Harry got along well with Evans, and became much more part of the family.

At Cardiff Art School, Harry met the Welsh painter Ceri Richards, a modernist painter and printmaker from a very cultured working-class background. Richards had had a solo exhibition at the Glynn Vivian Art Gallery in Swansea in 1930 and was well known for his Gower landscapes. When they first met, he told Harry to join a life class. Looking at a large naked female terrified the teenage Harry, he did not want to look too closely, and he ended up sitting as far away from his subject as possible. He drew the shoulders of the art students sitting in front of him closely, and the female nude at a distance. This perspective intrigued Richards more than any accomplished drawing of a female nude might have, and they became friendly. Richards became Harry's teacher and had a big influence on him. Harry contacted him when he returned from the war. By then, Ceri Richards was at Chelsea School of Art and recommended Harry go there, which is what he did. He managed to support himself with an ex-serviceman's grant but got nearly thrown out because the college did not care for his style and his technique, especially the fact that he used a lot of colour in his paintings. Through his cousin, Heinz Koppel, he met Oskar Kokoschka, who had taken over the studio of Josef Herman. Oskar agreed to tutor him, and thus a successful career as an artist and art teacher was kick-started.

Harry was finally accepted into the army in late 1944. At his interview with the recruiting sergeant, he was asked which part of the British Forces interested him most, and he replied that he wanted to join the infantry. 'Laddy, that can be arranged,' was the reply of the sergeant. Being finally able to fight fascism on the side of the allies was an important way of feeling accepted by British society and integrating fully into British life for many young male refugees. It also meant that their war experience from then onwards was part of a communal memory and not exceptional as their refugee experiences were. Harry joined the Queen's Own Royal West Kent Regiment when he was nearly 20 – older than most of the recruits. Nevertheless, he got on very well with other soldiers as he felt that they were all on the same side now.

Harry was still somewhat cynical, and thought the training was somewhat of a joke compared to the book he had read on the tactics and training regime of the Prussian army. No one seemed concerned about the fact he was German as there were so many foreign troops around; he was good at shooting, so he got specialist sniper and machine gun training. Harry wanted to join the Jewish Brigade that was fighting in Italy and his superiors agreed. He experienced an adventurous journey to Naples on a troop ship travelling from Ireland via Gibraltar: they were at sea for a fortnight and he felt sick a lot. His company was then transported by train and many soldiers swapped items of equipment for alcohol from the local Italians. Harry had thought that the war would carry on for a lot longer, and this was, of course, not the case. He ended up spending time guarding German prisoners of war rather than fighting. He then joined the Palestine Regiment, which was made up of men who had joined from what was then the British mandate of Palestine; most of them had trained in Egypt. The members of that regiment were all very physically fit, and many told stories of the most amazing adventures that they had experienced during the war. Some had fought for the International Brigades in Spain.

At the end of the war, the regiment was greeted with amazement by a group of Jewish survivors near the Italian border with Austria. Harry described how the Jewish survivors could not believe their eyes when they saw a regiment of the British army flying the Star of David flag. The soldiers gave the survivors their extra rations, cigarettes and chocolates, and this must have been the moment when Harry's two worlds collided: the world of the British army, which he had been so desperate to join, and the world of the mass murder that had been perpetrated in Central Europe. He had managed to escape from this fate while many of his friends and relatives had been murdered.

By this point, Harry had not seen his parents for years. While in Italy, he managed to get leave from the army and permission to travel to Switzerland to see them. Harry describes their meeting as '... embarrassing – they were not what I remembered – and they didn't seem that interested in what had happened to me.' Harry's experience is not untypical of many reunions between young refugees and their parents. He had last seen his mother and father in Berlin aged 15 and he was now a man in his early twenties. He had not heard from them or been able to communicate with them for six whole years. Harry felt that they sat like strangers in a restaurant at their first meeting. It is clear that both son and parents had had a lot of traumatic experiences and that it was very difficult to reconnect. In fact, Harry felt that they never managed to have a close parent-child relationship again.

Harry found that expressing himself through his art was one way to cope with the turmoil and trauma of his experiences. He and his cousin, Heinz Koppel, remained close, and Harry admired the delicacy of Koppel's work, and felt that Heinz should have received more recognition than he had. The Koppel family did not lose everything after fleeing National Socialism so Heinz was able to buy a farm in Mid Wales and build his own retreat and refuge. For Harry, his time in Wales became just one short stage in his long life. Harry had no financial support because his family had lost all their assets and wealth, and therefore he had to rely on his ability to earn a living through teaching art. He worked as an art teacher at schools in London and Reading, and then at a teacher training college in Manchester in the early 1960s. Later, he became Head of Painting at Lanchester Polytechnic, where he taught for nearly 20 years. Only after his retirement was he able to concentrate solely on his studio career. His paintings rarely have people as the subject, he focuses on interiors and objects. He rarely dated his paintings (causing problems for art critics and art buyers alike), believing that the observer should just focus on the content of the work and not the time it was created.

Refugee Girls on
Aberystwyth Promenade,
1939 (© Brian Pinsent)

Sir Alfred Dubs and Anita
H Grosz at the unveiling of
a sculpture commemorating
the Kindertransport at the
port of Harwich

REFUGEES IN WALES – NOW AND THEN

This book reflects an increasing interest in the history of refugees from Nazism in the UK since the turn of the millennium. To date this narrative has been largely dominated by the stories of refugees who resettled in England. This growth in interest has coincided with the arrival of new refugees from countries including Afghanistan, Syria and, most recently, Ukraine, leading to comparisons between those who fled from Nazi persecution and those who have escaped more recent oppression, persecution, and conflicts. There are some striking similarities between these situations as well as obvious differences.

In the 21st century, the UK government has not been generous in its support for sanctuary seekers compared to the governments of other wealthy European countries such as Sweden or Germany. Refugees are fleeing from an ever-increasing number of countries around the world, and there are different schemes for admitting those seeking sanctuary to the UK: some come as refugees, some come as asylum seekers. However, for example, while the British Vulnerable Persons Resettlement Scheme aimed to admit 20,000 – mainly Syrian – refugees between 2015 and 2020, Germany had already taken in over 600,000 Syrians by the end of 2015. Often it is neighbouring countries that take in the most refugees: over 1.3 million Syrians have been received in Turkey.

In the UK, the right to refuge has been repeatedly undermined, despite the country being signed up to the 1951 Refugee Convention. Over the last decade, sanctuary seekers have frequently been portrayed as just another group of immigrants in a context in which anti-immigrant rhetoric has been allowed to proliferate. Some sections of the media – as well as some politicians – have embraced anti-refugee sentiment for their own ends, rather than engaging with the fact-based discussions necessary to address and attempt to resolve such a difficult situation. During the Mediterranean refugee crisis, which came to the attention of the Western media in 2015, parallels were repeatedly drawn with the situation of the 1930s and 1940s. Some of these comparisons were aimed at the specific situation of child refugees rescued on a Kindertransport and compared the restrictions of 2015-16 unfavourably with the UK's generosity in 1938.

This led to many researchers pointing out that the situation in the 1930s was far from ideal. Many mistakes were made over 80 years ago, especially in relation to child refugees, and the decision to separate child refugees from their parents instead of admitting whole families can be seen in retrospect to be obviously wrong. Placements for the Kindertransportees were often not vetted and the adults involved had not received any training. As we have seen, the experiences these young refugees underwent in Wales varied, ranging from the rather idyllic, as in the case of Lia Lesser, to the abusive, as in the case of Susi Bechhöfer.

The Kindertransport scheme of 1938–39 demonstrated that despite a degree of anti-refugee rhetoric in the public domain, many people were willing to support refugees. As with the change of public mood in regard to Jewish refugees resulting from the November Pogrom in 1938, the death by drowning of a two-year old Syrian boy, Alan Kurdi, in September 2015, spurred many people in the UK into action, and led to a demand that the UK government should provide a structural framework for individuals or communities, rather than the state, to be able to help refugees. A policy change in 1938 enabled the establishment of the Kindertransport scheme; and a further policy change in 2016 initiated the Community Sponsorship Scheme. This scheme enabled communities to help find homes for those escaping a 21st century war. In both instances, the UK government largely relied on private citizens and community groups to support the refugees.

In 1938–39, the organisation of the transport, as well as the placements and the finances, had to be undertaken by non-governmental agencies. As discussed earlier in this book, the National Government in power at the time even demanded a £50 guarantee to be lodged to make sure that the young Kindertransport refugees would not be a financial burden to the state. Modern-day community sponsorship groups have to be able to demonstrate that accommodation, as well as educational and health services, is available in the local community setting and that those groups are able to support the refugees. A guarantee of £4,500 has to be raised by the community sponsor to cover potential expenses. (By coincidence, £50 in the late 1930s would be around £3600 today, so the sum is not too dissimilar.)

Of course, there are also differences. The Kindertransport scheme only allowed those under 18 years of age to escape to the UK; the Community Sponsorship Scheme is aimed at saving refugee families. The families are admitted under the Vulnerable Persons Resettlement Scheme (launched in January 2014) and are eligible for certain benefits and NHS services after their arrival (the health service did not exist in the 1930s, of course). But, in both instances, the UK government of the time relies on its citizens for organisational and financial support rather than offering more extensive support itself.

Over the last decade, the devolved government in Wales and local councils have been more supportive of providing sanctuary than the Westminster government. In 2010, Swansea became the second City of Sanctuary in the UK, and the first in Wales. Wales is also working towards becoming a Nation of Sanctuary. Placement of sanctuary seekers is not restricted to the urban areas and South Wales. Smaller Welsh counties have been at the forefront of providing support for refugees following the Mediterranean refugee crisis. In October 2015, Ceredigion County Council agreed to become a 'trailblazer' authority providing support for Syrian refugees, and a number of community sponsorship groups were successfully set up in different locations, including in more rural ones. Croeso Teifi in Cardigan, Aberaid in Aberystwyth and Croeso Menai in Gwynedd are organisations which have successfully resettled several families.

Some of the challenges refugees in Wales encounter today are similar to those encountered in the 1930s and 1940s, for example, two languages are used within Wales. I have not yet heard of any more recently arrived refugee becoming a Welsh-language campaigner like Kate Bosse-Griffiths; however, the children of a Syrian family resettled in Cardigan learnt both English and Welsh quickly and were happy to take part in a short TV documentary in which they demonstrated their Welsh language skills as well as their English. Most adult refugees attend English courses, and some have had Welsh lessons locally as well.

Many who found refuge in Wales in the 1930s did not know much about the country, or even of its existence, before they were resettled here. Ellen Davis' complete incomprehension of her situation and her destination, exemplified by the question 'What was Swansea?', illustrates this well. Despite the very different communication and information opportunities available today, refugees often still don't know anything about Wales, the different parts of Wales, or the existence of a distinct Welsh culture and language. Ghofran Hamza, a young woman originally from Syria, who was resettled with her family in Aberystwyth, stated in an interview in 2018:

'[After] a year of travelling, they told us that we're going to England. I said "Where... where is that? Where is that? I've never heard of that country!" Later on, we got to know that we were going to Ceredigion, so I looked up Ceredigion on Google. And when I saw the pictures – oh my god! – it's so beautiful! In Wales, it's different than England, you know, you see green everywhere, you see trees, you see wild places. The Welsh people are really lovely and when I walk, just like walking, even if I don't

234

meet people, just the feeling, the smells, the nature around us, the flowers I see in the houses. All these small things makes me so happy inside. And, I realised, like, even if it's a small place, you can't find everything but the love you find, you can't find it anywhere else, that's what's important and that's what we need.'

Ghofran Hamza's statement reminds us of what Josef Herman said about Ystradgynlais: 'It had all we needed.'

Many of the younger refugees appearing in this book described the tension between their educational ambition and the economic pressures to make a living as fast as possible after their arrival. Renate Collins was urged to get a job, which she did, but this left her with too little time and energy to continue her college course. She gave it up but felt very proud that despite this disappointment she managed to get a job at a company that later became British Airways. Many years later, Sulaiman, a young refugee woman, born in Manbli in the Aleppo region of Syria in 1993, talked about her exhaustion from working hard in a restaurant in Cardiff every day well into the early hours to support her family, while also trying to attend English classes in the mornings. In an interview she said:

'Sometimes, I used to fall asleep in the middle of the lesson. A colleague once took a video of me falling asleep in class and surprised me with the video afterwards. But day-by-day my English improved as a result of my interaction with restaurant customers.'

Sulaiman felt very proud when she was able to open her own restaurant, and when the college lecturer in whose classes she sometimes fell asleep visited the restaurant with a group of new students.

However, refugees also undergo many negative experiences. Lavan, a Sri Lankan Tamil from a Cardiff resident refugee family, describes the discrimination he experienced in his life:

'[...] Throughout my life even from when I was a little kid at school; just for being different I guess you do get a lot of discrimination. You get a lot of bullying and then, even in adult life now, there's probably discrimination at [my] workplace that I am not aware of, that is taking place. But growing up I always knew that that was the thing. It wasn't something new to me.'

Almost all refugees from Nazism whose stories are told in this book decided not to return to their originating countries after the Second World War. All that had made their former lives special, such as the religious and civic community, had been destroyed and many friends and family had either also left or had been murdered. Ultimately, they felt more comfortable in their new home. In this book, I discuss how Anton Hundsdorfer and Fanny Höchstetter considered a move back to Germany, but ultimately decided to stay in the UK. Some 21st century refugees find themselves in a similar situation. Natali Hadad, who was born in Homs in 1955 and worked as a microbiologist in Syria, was resettled with her daughter in Cardiff. When asked whether she thought she would return to Syria, she replied:

'I don't think I will go back to Syria as everybody has left. My parents passed away, my husband died, my friends and my relatives left the country. If I went back, I would be all alone. I have my daughter and grandchildren with me here and I am looking forward to meeting my sons in Europe and I feel happy and well settled in...'

When talking about the Kindertransport to students and members of the public, I used to point out the generosity of the British public and their willingness to provide places to live for over 10,000 child refugees within ten months in 1938–39. I used to say that I thought it unlikely that people would volunteer for such a role now. I was wrong. The start of Russia's invasion of Ukraine caused hundreds of thousands to flee their home country and engaged the compassion of many British people. However, the UK government is not making the process of escape to the UK easy. Compared to many neighbouring European countries, who allowed Ukrainians to cross their borders without a visa, Britain demands that Ukrainians apply for a permit – initially only granted under very specific circumstances, for example to people who had relatives in the UK willing to support them – as was true for a lot of refugees from the Third Reich.

However, as in the 1930s, the public have proved to be more generous than the government. Aead, a Syrian refugee who resettled in Aberystwyth with his wife and three children, is grateful to their community sponsor, which has supported the family using volunteer support workers and donations: 'I would like to say a special thank you to Aberaid, an organisation which helped me and my family with both psychological and social support.'

The war in Ukraine has spurred more private citizens into action and, due to public pressure, the Homes for Ukraine scheme was born, in which private hosts can apply to host Ukrainian refugees in their homes. Within a matter of weeks, over 80,000 potential hosts across the UK registered with the scheme. If Ukrainian refugees could be matched up with a British family that was willing to host them, they were eligible for a visa. The process has neither been fast nor trouble free, but sanctuary seekers from Ukraine have subsequently arrived in all the nations of the UK, including Wales.

Just two months after the invasion of Ukraine by Russia, on 22 April 2022, the Welsh government's Minister for Social Justice, Jane Hutt, gave an update on the Homes for Ukraine scheme across Wales, saying, '1,500 visas have been issued to date where the sponsor is from Wales; 1,100 have been sponsored by individuals in Wales and 390 are sponsored by the Welsh government as a super sponsor.' Those sponsored by the Welsh government have been accommodated in communal settings, such as Urdd centres, and are receiving support from different agencies to assist them with all aspects of settling in, like benefits and health and education services. Volunteers come to these centres to teach English and provide play opportunities for refugee children.

This shows that despite anti-refugee rhetoric from some political parties, individual politicians and parts of the media, many ordinary people are very keen to help. They are willing to give up space, time, and money. This does not mean that there are no challenges and difficulties regarding Ukrainian refugees. As with the Kindertransport hosts, the contemporary host families do not receive much if any preparation for their role. Checks are made regarding the suitability of offered housing and DBS checks are carried out on adult hosts, but, so far, there is little support or training to prepare the volunteers for the difficult role of hosting traumatised refugees who have escaped a war. In some cases, school places are not available quickly, and nor are English or Welsh lessons. There are delays with benefits and other services. Some Ukrainian refugee families have already had to leave their host families because of adjustment difficulties. Some hosts might have underestimated the complications of living with strangers in their own homes, and linguistic and cultural difficulties have sometimes proved too challenging. Many councils, including in Wales, are worried that a rising number of Ukrainian refugees might become homeless. The *Guardian* newspaper published an article on the problem in May 2022.

Finding refuge in Wales is – and has been – complicated and difficult; it is different for each specific group of people and even differs from individual to individual. Much has been written about the fact that the UK government which, of course, controls the visa system, has reacted in a more generous manner to the Ukrainian refugee crisis than to the Mediterranean refugee crisis. It is difficult to dismiss racism as a factor. Those seeking refuge in Wales in the 1930s also encountered discrimination, anti-refugee sentiment and, in their case, antisemitism, as Bea Green described in her story about the fellow student with Nazi sympathies. Nevertheless, overall, the narratives of refugees from National Socialism who came to Wales in the 1930s and 1940s are often very positive and express feelings of gratitude for being given refuge. This sentiment is also present in the stories of more recent refugees. But, as this book hopefully demonstrates, while there is often much to celebrate in these stories, it is important to understand their full complexity in order to fully appreciate the nature of the experience of attempting to find refuge in Wales and elsewhere.

Drawing of Czechoslovak State School, Llanwrtyd Wells, 1940
(© Bromsgrove School Archive. Reproduced by kind permission
of Bromsgrove School Archive)

EPILOGUE

This book contains the stories of those who fled to Wales to escape the Nazis. They reflect different experiences and sometimes they connect. I would like to single out Harry Weinberger's story which connects in many ways to the other stories in this book. Harry fled as a child refugee from Berlin on a Kindertransport, he worked on the Treforest Estate in a refugee-owned business, he was related to the Koppel family, and he must have known the Schoenmanns.

At the same time, each story is special. I have tried to choose stories that illustrate different aspects of the experience of refugees from National Socialism who settled in Wales. Again, Harry's efforts to join the British Army and fight the Nazis is an important experience that had to be included here. As is the experience of alienation from his parents after a period of separation of seven years and six years of no communication at all. What had happened could not be undone, and Harry's hope to establish the same close connection to his parents – as understandable as this hope was – proved unrealistic. It is a simple truth but you can never go back in history, only forward, and the best way to do this is to create something new.

This Harry did, and so did many other refugees. He was an artist, and his paintings are held in a number of collections in Wales and beyond. Other refugees became entrepreneurs or educators. Harry was not world famous, and for the most part led the ordinary life of an art teacher. Despite the fact that all refugees in this book had extraordinary stories to tell, most were not famous either and led, at least in parts, quite ordinary lives. It was the aim of this book to tell these stories to anyone who is interested in life in Wales. I hope the book shows how many of the refugees who resettled here in the

1930s and 1940s made Wales their home and are now as much part of the fabric of Welsh life as their neighbours. In time, the Syrians, Afghans and Ukrainians who followed them will be the same. Many of the refugees' children and grandchildren still live here now. Other refugees only stayed for a shorter time, such as Edith Tudor-Hart or the students of the Czechoslovak State School; however, their work and their memory will be part of Welsh culture forever.

ACKNOWLEDGEMENTS

Books like this are not written in isolation. As well as the decades I spent researching refugees from National Socialism, and the years I spent researching refugees from National Socialism in Wales, I had help from many people. First, I would like to thank my colleague Morris Brodie who started work with me in 2021 on the Refugees from National Socialism in Wales: Learning from the Past for the Future Project and managed to accomplish such a lot in a such a short space of time, and generously shared his research with me. This project was part of the Second World War and Holocaust Partnership Programme led by the Imperial War Museum, London, and funded by the National Heritage Lottery Fund. It included an exhibition on the subject first shown at the Aberystwyth Arts Centre during autumn/winter 2022–23 and at the Senedd and Pierhead Galleries in Cardiff in spring 2023.

I would also like to thank the film-maker Amy Daniel who worked with me on filmed interviews for the project, which also informed the book. I am grateful to my partner Nick Hubble for their encouragement and help in developing my writing, and to Honno Press and Caroline Oakley for their faith in my idea, and their editing, production and marketing skills.

I would also like to thank the following friends, family, colleagues, and collaborators (in alphabetical order):

Nathan Abrams, Tasha Alden, Tiffany Beebe, Monica Bohm-Duchen, Charmian Brinson, Renate Collins, Cathryn Charnell-White, Lucy Duncanson, Klavdija Erzen, Gábor Gelléri, Anthony Grenville, Jayne Gold, Anita H. Grosz. Heini Gruffudd, Alex Hammel, Max Hammel, Sara Hammel, Ghofran Hamza, Laura Henley Harrison, Andrew Hesketh, Joanne Hopkins, Rob

Jones, Gaby Koppel, Bea Lewkowicz, Alex Maws, Mo Ogier, Cai Parry-Jones, Brian Pinsent, George Schoenmann, Barbara Schreiber, Natasha Taylor, Janet Thomas, Stephanie Von Limpt-Homer, Moira Vincentelli, Heidi Wiener, the members and trustees of Aberaid, my students and colleagues at Aberystwyth University and especially at the Centre for the Movement of People (CMOP), the members of the Research Centre for German and Austrian Exile Studies and the Gesellschaft für Exilforschung, the members and elders of St. David's Church in Aberystwyth, the Syrian community in Aberystwyth.

I used the following sources for my research on the stories of the men, woman and children who fled to Wales to escape the Nazis (in chapter order):

https://www.ajrrefugeevoices.org.uk/
[last accessed 1 February 2022]
Andrea Hammel, 'I remember their labels round their necks: Britain and the Kindertransport', in Lawson and Pearce (eds), *The Palgrave Handbook on Britain and the Holocaust*, 2020
Andrea Hammel, 'Narrating the Margins and the Center: Kindertransportees' Stories of National and Religious Belonging', *Shofar*, Purdue University Press, Fall 2019
Correspondence of Eva Mosbacher who escaped on a Kindertransport:
http://www.kindertransport.eu/familie-mosbacher/ [last accessed 15 July 2022]

Julian Borger, 'Refugees bring hope, not trouble – my father's story is proof of that'. *The Guardian*, 7 September 2015, https://www.theguardian.com/commentisfree/2015/sep/07/father-refugee-family-nazis-syria [last accessed 12 December 2021]
Julian Borger, 'I seek a kind person': the Guardian ad that saved

my Jewish father from the Nazis', *The Guardian*, 6 May 2021, https://www.theguardian.com/media/2021/may/06/guardian-200-ad-that-saved-jewish-father-from-nazis
Interview with Julian Borger, conducted by Andrea Hammel, 13 May 2021

Josef Herman, *Notes from a Welsh Diary*, Free Association Books, 1988
Josef Herman, *Related Highlights: Notes from an Artist's Diary*, Seren, 2002
Monica Bohm-Duchen, *The Art and Life of Josef Herman*, Lund Humphries, 2009

Edith Tudor-Hart, *In the Shadow of Tyranny*, ed. Duncan Forbes, Hatje Cantz Verlag, 2013
Peter Stephan Jungk, *Die Dunkelkammern der Edith Tudor-Hart*, Fischer Taschenbuch, 2017

Heini Gruffudd, *A Haven from Hitler*, Y Lolfa, 2014
Interview with Heini Gruffudd, conducted by Morris Brodie and Andrea Hammel, 23 September 2021

Transcript of the oral history interview with George Schoenmann, conducted by Mike Hawkins, Jewish History Association of South Wales, 20 September 2018, selected audio clips available
https://www.peoplescollection.wales/items/1221501
[last accessed 27 June 2022]

Chana Schütz and Hermann Simon, *Heinz Koppel: Ein Künstler zwischen Berlin und Wales*, VBB, 2009
Interview with Gaby Koppel, conducted by Morris Brodie and Andrea Hammel, 1 February 2022

Interview with Ernie Hunter, son of Anton Hundsdorfer and Fanny Höchstetter, conducted by Morris Brodie and Andrea Hammel, 19 January 2022

Gerhard Oertel (1995) 'Trade union activity of German refugees during the second world war in the forestry of North Wales: Recollections of personal experiences', *Immigrants & Minorities: Historical Studies in Ethnicity, Migration and Diaspora*, 14:3, 257–264, DOI:10.1080/02619288.1995.9974866

Interview with Bea Green, 12 July 1996
https://www.iwm.org.uk/collections/item/object/80016229
[last accessed 10 January 2022]

Da'at ha-hevrah, Erich Roper (Yis'akhar Roper), Willy Braun (Ze'ev Hayim Broyn), Bernhard Liwerant (Binyamin Liverant), editors, 2 February 1940. In Hebrew, German and English

John Edelnand, 'There's a Welcome in the Hillside', Abergele Field Club and Historical Society, Review No. 6, 1987

Interview with Arieh Handler, AJR Refugee Voices Testimony interview (RV25). Arieh Handler was interviewed by Bea Lewkowicz on 9 July 2003

Andrew D. Hesketh, '"Did you come here to die?" The Gwrych Castle Hachshara 1939–1941', unpublished manuscript, monograph forthcoming with University of Wales Press in 2024

Laura Henley Harrison, 'Where Do We Go From Here? Sheltering Jewish Refugees in Welsh Castles During the Second World War and How We Can Continue to Keep a Welcome in the Hillside', unpublished manuscript.

Jeremy Josephs with Susi Bechhöfer, *Rosa's Child*, IB Tauris, 1999

Interview with Susi Bechhöfer, conducted by Andrea Hammel, 14 June 2012

Susi Bechhöfer, *Rosa*, Christians Aware, 2016

Martin Modlinger, 'You can't change names and feel the same': The

Kindertransport Experience of Susi Bechhöfer in W. G. Sebald's *Austerlitz*' in Andrea Hammel and Bea Lewskowicz (eds), *The Kindertransport to Britain 1938/39: New Perspectives*, Brill, 2012.

Interview with William Dieneman, conducted by Andrea Hammel, 14 June 2011
https://pure.aber.ac.uk/portal/files/28123277/interview_with_william_dieneman.pdf

Interview with Renate Collins, conducted by Andrea Hammel, 20 May 2021
That's Life with Esther Rantzen, 1988,
https://www.youtube.com/watch?v=OqqbM1B-mPY

Ellen Davis, *Kerry's Children*, Seren, 2004
Interview with Ellen Davis, conducted by Andrea Hammel, 12 May 2012

Interview with Herbert Patrick Anderson, 25 November 1998
https://www.iwm.org.uk/collections/item/object/80017603
[last accessed 3 January 2022]

Interview with Harry Weinberger, 12 January 1995 and 17 March 1995
https://sounds.bl.uk/Oral-history/Art/021M-C0466X0037XX-0500V0 [last accessed 1 February 2022]

https://museum.wales/refugee-wales/stories
[last accessed 26 June 2022]
http://onestorymanyvoices.iwm.org.uk/stories/what-can-you-do
[last accessed 27 June 2022]
https://www.baysideradio.co.uk/news/homes-for-ukraine-scheme-growing-in-wales-says-minister-6089
[last accessed 27 June 2022]

https://www.gov.uk/government/publications/uk-resettlement-schemes-factsheet-march-2021/vulnerable-persons-and-vulnerable-childrens-resettlement-schemes-factsheet-march-2021 [last accessed 15 July 2022]